ספר איוב THE BOOK OF JOB

ספר איוב

with introductions by

MOSHE GREENBERG

JONAS C. GREENFIELD

NAHUM M. SARNA

Philadelphia 5740 / 1980

THE BOOK OF JOB

A NEW TRANSLATION ACCORDING TO THE TRADITIONAL HEBREW TEXT

THE JEWISH PUBLICATION SOCIETY OF AMERICA

Manufactured in the United States of America

Library of Congress Cataloging in Publication Data
Bible. O. T. Job. Hebrew. 1980. The book of Job ספר איוב
Job in English and Hebrew; introductory material in English.
I. Jewish Publication Society of America. II. Bible. O. T. Job. English. Jewish Publication Society. 1980. III. Title. IV. Title: Sefer Iyov.
BS1412 1980 223'.1044 79-25323
ISBN 0-8276-0172-7

Designed by Adrianne Onderdonk Dudden

Contents

Preface

In 1966 The Jewish Publication Society of America set up a committee of translators for *Kethubim (The Writings)*—the third part of the Hebrew Bible. The committee comprised Professors Moshe Greenberg (now of the Hebrew University), Jonas C. Greenfield (now of the Hebrew University), and Nahum M. Sarna of Brandeis University. Associated with them were Rabbis Saul Leeman, Martin Rozenberg, and David S. Shapiro of the three sections of organized religious Jewish life in America. Dr. Chaim Potok served as secretary of the committee.

The present English rendering of Job—published now in advance of its inclusion in the forthcoming edition of the committee's *Kethubim*—is a new version, not a revision of an earlier translation. It is based on the received (Masoretic) Hebrew text —its consonants, vowels, and syntactical divisions, although on occasion the traditional accentuation has been disregarded in favor of an alternative construction of a verse that appeared to yield a better sense. Such departures from the accentuation were made by many earlier Jewish commentators and translators.

The entire gamut of Job interpretation, from ancient to modern times, Jewish and non-Jewish, has been consulted. The results of modern study of the languages and cultures of the ancient Near East have been brought to bear on the biblical word wherever possible. In judging between alternatives, however, just as antiquity was not in itself a disqualification, so modernity was not in itself a recommendation. When the present translation diverges from recent renderings (as it frequently does), this is due as much to our judgment that certain innovations, though interesting, are too speculative for adoption in the present state of knowledge, as to our commitment to the received Hebrew text (a commitment not made by most recent translations).

For many passages, our as yet imperfect understanding of the language of the Bible or what appears to be some disorder in the Hebrew text makes sure translation impossible. Our uncertainty is indicated in a note, and alternative renderings have sometimes been offered where the Hebrew permits them. However, emendations of the text have not been proposed and notes have been kept to a minimum.

The style of the translation is modern literary English. An effort has been made to retain the imagery of the Hebrew rather than to render it by English equivalents and approximations alien to the biblical world.

Consistency in rendering Hebrew terms was an aim but not an

unqualified rule. Where its employment would have resulted in encumbered or awkward language it was abandoned.

The interpretation of the text and meaning of Job posed extraordinary, to us at times insuperable, difficulties. We know, too, that we have not conveyed the fullness of the Hebrew, with its ambiguities, its overtones, and the richness of meaning it carries from centuries of use. Yet we do hope to have transmitted something of the directness, the simplicity, and the power that are so essential to the sublimity of the Hebrew Book of Job.

Committee of Translators
Kethubim (The Writings)

Tammuz 5739 / July 1979

The Book of Job: General Introduction

NAHUM M. SARNA

THE NAME

Biblical tradition has failed to preserve the name of the incomparable genius who was the author of the Book of Job. Not surprisingly, some rabbinic teachers felt that only one of the stature of Moses himself was worthy to be connected with so sublime and consummate a work (Baba Batra 14b). Even its original title is uncertain. The Book of Job (*Sefer Iyyob, Iyyob* for short) is the sole name that has come down to us, which is only fitting, since its towering hero dominates the work from first to last.

The interpretation of the name itself is not at all certain. One is tempted, of course, to invest it with symbolic meaning, and to connect the Hebrew *Iyyob* with the stem *'YB,* "to be hostile," "to suffer hostility," which is exactly what the rabbis of the Talmud did, albeit playfully (Baba Batra 16a; Niddah 52a). But there is another, more likely, possibility. The name Job, in an early Semitic form *('ay'ab),* has been widely attested in the ancient Near East over a long period of time. It was borne by a Canaanite chief as early as around 2000 B.C.E., as is mentioned in an Egyptian Execration text. It also belonged to a prince of Ashtaroth in the Bashan, according to an Amarna Letter (256.6), and various other personalities of the same name are recorded in cuneiform texts from Mari and Alalakh, in the alphabetic texts from Ugarit, and in South Arabian and Thamudic inscriptions. The manner of writing "Job" in cuneiform suggests that it is to be interpreted as a compound of *'ay* and *'ab,* meaning, "Where is the [divine] Father?"—an appellation not inappropriate for that anguished biblical soul who cries out for divine justice.

ITS PLACE IN THE CANON

In spite of the daring and controversial nature of its contents, the propriety of including the Book of Job in the biblical canon seems never to have been called into question. It has always occupied an honored place in *Kethubim,* the third section of the Hebrew Scriptures. Because of its size, Job joined Psalms and Proverbs to form "the great writings" (Berakhot 57b). The oldest surviving list of *Kethubim* places the book between these two (Baba Batra 14b; Gittin 35a), but offers no explanation for this order. Perhaps a theory of chronological sequence was the determining factor, or perhaps it was to allow books ascribed to Solomon to be clustered together thereafter. At any rate, it appears thus in the

Aleppo Codex (10th century C.E.), the Leningrad Codex B (1008 C.E.), and also, generally, in the Spanish Bible Codices. Ashkenazi manuscripts and the printed editions, however, place Job after Proverbs.

THE TARGUMS TO JOB

Despite its difficult language, the popularity of the book must always have been considerable, for translations into other languages already existed in the time of the Second Temple. A famous report of one such translation comes from the writings of the Tanna R. Yose son of Halafta, who was a student of R. Akiba (d. 135 C.E.). He relates that his father, Halafta, once went to visit Rabban Gamaliel II, in Tiberias, and found him reading a Targum scroll of Job. Thereupon, Halafta recalled a story about Rabban Gamaliel I, who was once sitting on a step on the Temple mount when a translation of Job was brought before him. Displeased, he ordered that it be secreted under a row of stones (Tosefta Shabbat xiii, 2).

Unfortunately, neither the language of the translation, whether Aramaic or Greek, nor the reason for the patriarch's displeasure has been preserved. But the story has acquired added interest in light of the Aramaic Targum to the Book of Job that turned up in Cave XI at Qumran from the library of the sect that occupied the site in the last centuries of the Second Temple. There is no way of knowing, of course, if any connection exists between this version and the one seen by Gamaliel I. The Qumran document is very fragmentary, and the first sixteen chapters are missing. Nevertheless, what has remained indicates that it was made from a Hebrew text remarkably close to our received text. There is no connection between these ancient Targums and the present Aramaic version, printed in the rabbinic Bibles, which derives from the early Middle Ages.

THE NARRATIVE BACKGROUND

The Book of Job is made up of two distinct parts, prose and poetry. The author has chosen the prose style as the vehicle for the narrative Prologue (chs. 1–2) and Epilogue (42.7–17) that encase the main body of the work, which is the poetic disputation (3.1–42.6). The story is simple. Job is a saintly man of considerable means. Because the Accuser (the "Satan") challenges the disinterested nature of his piety before the heavenly assembly, God permits Job to be tested by a series of disasters that deprive him of his children, strip him of his worldly possessions, and leave him the victim of some horrible skin disease. Despite this crushing burden of misfortune, no word of impiety, of questioning God's actions, escapes his lips.

When his wife suggests that he renounce God and thereby put an end to his sufferings, he soundly rebukes her, and reaffirms his simple, unshakable faith: "Should we accept only good from God and not accept evil?" he asks. Three of his friends learn of his unutterable misery, and they travel from their respective lands to be with him and to console him. After a week of uninterrupted, somber, and obviously reflective silence, our hero finally unburdens himself, and he curses the day of his birth.

The Epilogue is quite brief. It opens with the implication that Job and his friends have engaged in serious discussion. God takes the side of Job, who now becomes an intercessor on behalf of his friends. He is then doubly recompensed by God for all his losses, becomes the father of more children, and lives to a ripe old age, enjoying the company of his great-grandchildren.

There is clearly some discrepancy between the stoic figure of the Narrative and the fiercely argumentative, accusatory Job of the Poem. The explanation is not hard to find. The author has made use of an earlier story for his own theological-philosophical purposes. Who is this man named Job? All we know is that he lives in the land of Uz. Neither the name of his father nor any chronological information is given.

Where the text fails us, speculation fills the void. The Greek translation bears an addendum identifying Job with Jobab son of Zerah, the second king of Edom (Gen. 36.33), and this fancy must have circulated among the Jews of the Middle Ages, for Abraham ibn Ezra (1092–1167) takes pains to refute it. In talmudic literature, the entire spectrum of chronological possibility is covered, beginning with the time of Abraham and continuing into the age of Jacob (according to some, Job was actually the patriarch's son-in-law) and projecting him as a contemporary of Moses, the Judges, Solomon, Nebuchadnezzar, Ahasuerus, and as one of the returnees from the Babylonian Exile (Baba Batra 16a; P. Sotah 5.6 (8), 20[c]). Unable to identify the hero unequivocally, one critical Amora, in desperation, actually declared Job to be a fictitious character, and the book to be an allegory composed for didactic purposes (Baba Batra 15a). Yet the prophet Ezekiel knew of a Job who, together with Noah and Daniel, was a classic exemplar of true righteousness (Ezek. 14.14, 20). This citation takes on added significance in light of the discovery of an Ugaritic text concerning a certain Danel, an honest judge, famous for his solicitous care of the widow and the orphan. It seems certain that Ezekiel was aware of some tale about an ancient worthy named Job who was a paradigm of integrity.

How much of the Narrative of Job is indebted to an ancient legend? Did our author draw upon a well-known tale on which to base his present text? First, it should be stressed that the two parts of the Narrative, or Framework, of the poem demonstrably belong to a single composition. In both, the hero is cited as "My servant Job," and, in both, he plays the role of intercessor, presenting burnt offerings to assuage God's anger. The order in which Job's material belongings are listed is the same in both sections, and the enumeration of his restored and redoubled possessions presupposes a knowledge of the Prologue. The three friends are mentioned in identical order in both parts, and in neither does the name of Elihu appear. The narrative Prologue and Epilogue thus form a unity, and constitute the tale on which the philosopher-poet hangs his discourse.

The social and religious setting of the story is unmistakably patriarchial—Job is a figure whose wealth is measured in terms of cattle and slaves. Sabeans and Chaldeans are not yet organized into kingdoms, but are still wild, nomadic tribes. Religion knows no priesthood or central shrine, only private sacrifice. Job's longevity recalls that of the pre-Mosaic period, and he dies, like Abraham (Gen. 25.8) and Isaac (Gen. 35.29), "old and contented." The patriarchal setting really adds nothing to our understanding of the book's theme, and for this reason alone we can safely assume that it is a vestigial remnant from an original tale, probably the one that Ezekiel had in mind. This case is strengthened by the presence of several other features peculiar to the Narrative.

The series of misfortunes that beset Job are presented in a way that bespeaks a carefully designed, symmetrical, literary arrangement. The structural pattern is reminiscent of that underlying the Ten Plagues. There are three groups of two afflictions each, in which the first blow falls on livestock and the second on human beings. The cause of each series is alternatively human and divine, and the whole culminates in a climactic divinely-wrought seventh calamity.

And here another singularity appears: the extensive use of the number seven. Job has seven sons; his children celebrate seven-day feasts; he experiences seven disasters; his friends maintain a silent vigil of seven days and seven nights, and, when it is all over, they offer seven bulls and seven rams. It is not coincidental that Job has seven sons and three daughters; this is a characteristically epic and mythological motif. In the Ugaritic texts, King Keret is said to have begotten seven sons, while the god Baal, like Job, sired three daughters as well. Triads of daughters are a common motif, especially in Greek mythology. Moreover, the names of Job's daughters are given, whereas the sons remain anonymous, precisely the case as with Baal's children. In this respect, too, the social milieu reflects the epic tradition. Feminine pulchritude is exalted, the girls participate in the feasts alongside their brothers, and, together with them, receive an inheritance, quite contrary to the practice in Israel (Num. 27.8).

Finally, the Narrative of Job contains some mythological elements comprising two scenes describing the assembly of the heavenly host, in which God and Satan are the principal actors. The image of Satan here is not that of the later literature. He is simply the Adversary, who enjoys no independence of action and who cannot do his evil work without permission from God. And "Satan" is not yet a proper name, for it invariably occurs with the definite article.

All in all, there is a plethora of multifaceted evidence for concluding that behind the narrative Framework lies an ancient tale, from which many details have been incorporated intact into the prose sections of the present Book of Job.

The Language of the Book

JONAS C. GREENFIELD

The Book of Job has posed more difficulties for translators and commentators than any other part of the Hebrew Bible. Its language is often difficult; there are lines whose interpretation depends entirely on the translator's understanding of the context and his ability to make the best of what is preserved in the text.

The difficulties, on the whole, are found in the poetic part of the book. The Framework story (chs. 1–2, 42.7–17) is told in a classical prose style. It has a strong patriarchal coloring, evident not only in the description of Job's way of life but also in the choice of words dealing with his age (Job 42.17, cf. Gen. 35.29) and wealth (Job 1.3, cf. Gen. 26.14), and it reflects epic elements that must go back to an earlier prose tale. By his skillful choice of words and phrases, the author has provided allusions to various biblical narratives; through the use of such literary devices as assonance, alliteration, and parallelism, he has lifted the prose away from the merely descriptive. Yet we are informed by recent research—for example, the careful study of the use of various words (*qabbel,* "to accept," 2.10), turns of phrase (*'îš hāyā . . . ušmō,* "there was a man . . . named," 1.1), and choice of preposition (*yitpallel 'al,* "will pray for," 42.8)—that the present form of the prose Framework was composed in the Persian period.

The poetic part of Job (chs. 3–42.6) has provided the rabbis in the Talmud and Midrash with many passages whose obscurity made them fertile soil for contradictory interpretations. The early translator into Greek no longer understood many passages, and so omitted them; the original version of the Septuagint is about a hundred verses shorter than the later edition and was based, in all likelihood, on a text in the old Hebrew script. Comparison with the Latin, Greek, and Syriac versions, as well as with the traditional Targum, shows that the ancients were far from agreement as to the reading and meaning of those same words and passages about which we turn to them for enlightenment today. Indeed, their struggle with the Hebrew text is apparent; they often have recourse to the same sort of paraphrase or contextual translation on which modern translators, equipped with the best philological tools, must rely. A Job Targum was recently discovered at Qumran, near the Dead Sea. At times it offers two translations for the same Hebrew word (39.21); thus *yāśîś* is translated *yrwṭ,* "he will run," and *yḥd',* "he will rejoice."

The reason for all this confusion is not hard to find. Job has more hapax legomena and rare words than any other book in the Hebrew Bible. The language is exceptionally rich. There is an unusual number of synonyms and descriptive words; names of animals, minerals, and stars; terms from the fields of mining and hunting. The detailed anatomy of exotic beasts was known to the author, as was the technical language of the law. Alongside words that are easily recognizable are others that are not known; even in juxtaposition, their overall meaning is unfamiliar and not readily comprehensible. And another element characteristic of this book is the frequent use of part of a verse familiar to the reader from elsewhere in the Bible (although it is possible that to the author this was simply a familiar hymnic phrase) together with a verse whose meaning is unclear.

These and other considerations have led scholars to propose a variety of theories as to the origin of the Book of Job. Some have taken their cue from the medieval commentator Abraham ibn Ezra, who thought that Job was translated from another language (see his comment on 2.11) and was therefore difficult to understand. Both Aramaic and Arabic have been put forward as the book's original language. It cannot be denied that the Aramaic influence in the text is strong, especially in the Elihu chapters (32–37), for many of the hapax legomena and rare words are clearly identifiable as Aramaic, or Aramaic provides the clue to their interpretation—for example, *ḥawweh,* "to tell," *śāhēd,* "witness," and *geled,* "skin." Grammatical forms, such as the masculine plural (*-īn,* rather than the usual Hebrew form *-īm,* in *millīn,* "words," and *ḥayyīn,* "life") and *minhem,* "from them," instead of *mehem*, may be identified as Aramaic in origin.

The complex arguments for an Aramaic origin of Job, however, have not supplied the key for unlocking the difficulties of the text. Nor is that key the use—indeed, the abuse—of the vast resources of the Arabic lexicon. There are various words which, when taken in their Arabic meaning, make good sense in context —thus, on the basis of Arabic cognates, the verbs *'śh* and *'ṭp* in Job 23.9 may be interpreted as "to turn"—and there are other examples of the use of Arabic; but many scholars are wary of relying too heavily on this element as an aid to the understanding of the Book of Job.

The use of philological information garnered from Canaanite epigraphic sources—Ugaritic texts and Phoenician inscriptions— has been hailed in some quarters. But these texts have not greatly advanced the understanding of the poetic portion of Job. Random phrases, such as *mibbĕkī nĕhārōt,* "sources of the streams" (28.11), and *nibĕkē yam,* "sources of the sea" (38.16), have been clarified. Of greater importance, however, is the fact that the Canaanite material has enabled scholars to appreciate more fully the mythological background of such imagery as the battle with the sea (26.12–13), the role of the Rephaim (26.5), and the references to the sea and the dragon (7.12), for material from such sources may have been used or quoted in Job.

No simple comprehensive answer has yet been found to account for the linguistic difficulties in Job. The author(s) not only had a rich vocabulary in Hebrew but was also familiar with literature that was to become part of the biblical corpus (Psalms, Isaiah), with ancient material now lost to us, and with neighboring dialects, having drawn upon all these to enrich the language of the book's protagonists, who are given tribal designations that would indicate non-Israelite origin.

It has been suggested that the Aramaic flavor of a good part of the book is a result of the Kedemite origin attributed to Job and his friends. Kedem is the region of the middle Euphrates, and the tribes that settled there spoke Aramaic during and after the period of the First Temple; the area in which Job lived was contiguous to the desert areas inhabited by Arab tribes. Thus, local dialects may have provided some elements of speech that would have given the book a stamp of authenticity for its contemporary readers but that have added to the difficulty of transmitting a text which, for its later readers and translators, still contains many mysteries.

Reflections on Job's Theology

MOSHE GREENBERG

Job is a book not so much about God's justice as about the transformation of a man whose piety and view of the world were formed in a setting of wealth and happiness, and into whose life burst calamities that put an end to both. How can piety nurtured in prosperity prove truly deep-rooted and disinterested, and not merely a spiritual adjunct of good fortune ("God has been good to me so I am faithful to Him")? Can a man pious in prosperity remain pious when he is cut down by anarchical events that belie his orderly view of the world? The Book of Job tells how one man suddenly awakened to the anarchy rampant in the world, yet his attachment to God outlived the ruin of his tidy system.

Job is a pious believer who is struck by misfortune so great that it cannot be explained in the usual way as a prompting to repentance, a warning, let alone a punishment (the arguments later addressed to him by his friends). His piety is great enough to accept the misfortune without rebelling against God: "Should we accept only good from God and not accept evil?" (1.10). But his inability, during seven days of grief in the company of his silent friends, to find a reasonable relation between the misfortune and the moral state of its victims (himself and his children) opens Job's eyes to the fact that in the world at large the same lack of relation prevails (9.22–24; 12.6–9; 21.7–34). Until then, the crying contradiction between the idea of a just order and the reality of individual destinies had, because of his prosperity, hardly been visible to Job. He may not have been as simple as his friends, but neither was he more perceptive than Elihu, who, at the end (chs. 32–37), offers those above-mentioned explanations of misfortune. But Job now knows their absurdity and their inadequacy to save a reasonable divine order according to human standards of morality.

The Prologue of the book, telling of Satan's wager and the subsequent disaster that befell Job, has been a scandal to many readers. But the Prologue is necessary, first of all, to establish Job's righteousness. To depict the effect of dire misfortune that demolishes the faith of a perfectly blameless man in a just divine order is the author's purpose. The book is not merely an exposition of ideas, a theological argument, but the portrayal of a spiritual journey from simple piety to the sudden painful awareness and eventual acceptance of the fact that inexplicable misfortune is the lot of man. Without the Prologue we should lack the essential knowledge that Job's misfortune really made no sense; without the Prologue the friends' arguments that misfortune indicates sin would be plausible, and Job's resistance to them liable to be construed as moral arrogance. The Prologue convinces us from the outset of Job's integrity, hence we can never side with the friends. For Job is a paradigm ("He never was or existed," says a talmudic rabbi, "except as an example" [Baba Batra 15a]). He personifies every pious man who, when confronted with an absurd disaster, is too honest to lie in order to justify God. The author must convince his readers that Job's self-estimation is correct, and that therefore his view of moral disorder in God's management of the world is warranted. That is one purpose of the Prologue.

Satan's wager and God's assent to it dramatize a terrible quandary of faith: a pious man whose life has always been placid can never know whether his faith in God is more than an interested bargain—a convenience that has worked to his benefit—unless it is tested by events that defy the postulate of a divine moral order. Only when unreasonable misfortune erupts into a man's life can he come to know the basis of his relation to God, thus allaying doubts (personified here by Satan) that both he and others must harbor toward his faith. To conquer these doubts by demonstrating that disinterested devotion to God can indeed exist is necessary for man's spiritual well-being; God's acquiescence in Satan's wager expresses this necessity. The terrible paradox is that no righteous man can measure his love of God unless he suffers a fate befitting the wicked.

The speeches of Job reveal the collapse of his former outlook. For the first time in his life he has become aware of the prevalence of disorder in the government of the world. In his former state of well-being, Job would hardly have countenanced in himself or in others a death wish; in his misfortune, however, he expresses it vehemently (3.11–23). Could Job, in his prosperity, have appreciated the anguish of victims of senseless misfortune, or have regarded God as an enemy of man (7.17–21; 9.13–24; 16.9–14; 12.5)? Job would previously have responded to despair of God as his friends and Elihu responded to him in his misery and despair. For Job's friends were his peers ideologically no less than socially; he belonged to their circle both in deed and in creed. A chasm opened between him and them only because of a disaster that Job alone knew to be undeserved.

Job's pathetic appeals for a bill of indictment (10.2; 13.18ff.; 23.1ff.; 31.35f.) belong to the context of the neat, orderly system in which he had once believed. One wonders whether such repeated affirmations of his innocence are not aimed as much toward his friends as toward God, in an effort to break down their complacency. But since his friends neither have undergone his suffering nor share his confidence in his own righteousness, they will not question the validity or give up the security of their system.

Though Job never tires of denouncing the inadequacy of his former concept of the divine government (a concept which his friends still adhere to), his complaints are addressed to God. The orderly fabric of his life has been irreparably rent, yet his relation to God persists. We shall soon consider how that could be.

The outcome of the drama is that the collapse of a complacent view of the divine economy can be overcome. For Job this came about through a sudden overwhelming awareness of the complexity of God's manifestation in reasonless phenomena of nature. Job's flood of insight comes in a storm (סערה)—we may suppose, through the experience of its awesomeness. One may compare and contrast the midrashic word play that has Job hearing God's answer out of a "hair" (שערה), from contemplation of a microcosm. The grand vista of nature opens before Job, and it reveals the working of God in a realm other than man's moral order. Job responds to, and thus gets a response from, the numinous presence underlying the whole panorama; he hears God's voice in the storm. The fault in the moral order—the plane on which God and man interact—is subsumed under the totality of God's work, not all of which is reasonable. Senseless calamity loses some of its demoralizing effect when morale does not depend entirely on the comprehensibility of the phenomena but, rather, on the conviction that they are pervaded by the presence of God. As nature shows, this does not necessarily mean that they are sensible and intelligible.

It has been objected that God's speeches (chs. 38–41) are irrelevant to Job's challenge. God—the objection runs—asserts His power in reply to a challenge to His moral government. But this sets up a false dichotomy. To be sure, God's examples from nature are exhibitions of His power, but they are also exhibitions of His wisdom and His providence for His creatures (38.27; 39.1–4; 26). Through nature, God reveals Himself to Job as both purposive and nonpurposive, playful and uncanny, as evidenced by the monsters He created. To study nature is to perceive the complexity, the unity of contraries, in God's attributes, and the inadequacy of human reason to explain His behavior, not the least in His dealings with man.

For it may be inferred that in God's dealings with man, this complexity is also present—a unity of opposites: reasonability, justice, playfulness, uncanniness (the latter appearing demonic in the short view). When Job recognizes in the God of nature, with His fullness of attributes, the very same God revealed in his own individual destiny, the tumult in his soul is stilled. He has fathomed the truth concerning God's character; he is no longer tortured by a concept that fails to account for the phenomena, as did his former notion of God's orderly working (42.1–6).

If God is a combination of divergent attributes, and is a cause of misfortune, why does Job not reject Him?

What had Job known of God in his former happy state? He had known Him as a conferrer of order and good. Basking in His light, Job's life had been suffused with blessings (29.2–5). No later evidence to the contrary could wipe out Job's knowledge of God's benignity gained from personal experience. Job calls that former knowledge of God a "hearing," while his latter knowledge, earned through suffering, is a "seeing" (42.5); that is, the latter knowledge gained about God is to the former as seeing is to hearing—far more comprehensive and adequate. Formerly, Job had only a limited notion of God's nature—as a benign, constructive factor in his life, "good" in terms of human morality. At that time, any evidence that ran against this conception of God was peripheral: it lay outside Job's focus. He assumed that it too could somehow be contained in his view of the divine moral order, but nothing pressed him to look the uncongenial facts in the face.

But misfortune moved the periphery into the center, and the perplexity that ensued is a testimony to Job's piety, for he was not transformed by senseless misfortune into a scoffer—a denier of God—but, instead, thrown into confusion. His experience of God in good times had left on him an indelible conviction of God's goodness that clashed with the new, equally strong evidence of God's enmity. Though one contradicted the other, Job experienced both as the work of God, and did not forget the first (as did his wife) when the second overtook him.

The author of Job had a dedication to theological honesty and a passion to teach the reality of God's relation to man that are unique in the Bible.* Job cannot rest after the collapse of his old outlook until he has come to a better one, more congruent with the facts of experience. How highly the author prizes right knowledge of God is revealed by his final estimate of Job's friends. Although they argued in evident good faith, in the Epilogue God is angry at them and declares them in need of forgiveness (42.7–8). Wrong thinking about God is reprehensible. One might say that an aim of the author of Job is to warn men away from such culpable misconceptions. After Job, God is not willing to be conceived of in the friends' terms; after Job, such views are abhorrent to Him.

To the very end, Job remains ignorant of the true cause of his misfortunes, for he never learns of Satan's wager. Job appears to have found consolation in his realization of the complexity of God, but the reader knows more: he knows that Job's suffering was the result of a divine bet on Job's disinterested piety.

Why couldn't Job, like Abraham, have been told at the end that the entire event was a trial, and have heard, as did Abraham, "Now I know that you fear God" (Gen. 22.12)?

From the Epilogue, it is clear that God's vindication of Job's honesty, proven in his passionate recriminations against God and against his friends' simplistic theories, is more important for Job than knowing the reason for his suffering. The Epilogue shows Job satisfied by the divine assurance that his friends' arguments were specious, as he had always asserted (13.7–10; 19.22–29; 42.7–9). Beyond that God does not go in revealing to Job the cause of his suffering.

Abraham's case is not identical to Job's, for, in the end, Abraham did not sacrifice Isaac, while Job lost all his children and his possessions. It was dreadful enough for Abraham to learn that his God was capable of subjecting His followers to trials that brought them to the verge of disaster, even though He rescued them at the last moment. For Job to have learned that his family and his possessions had been annihilated because of a mere wager with Satan—that he had been a pawn in a celestial game—would have been far harder to accept than was the mystery of a God part known, part hidden, whose overall work is nevertheless good. For it is easier to bear a mixture of benignity and

**Kohelet shares with Job the clear-eyed vision of a flawed moral governance of the world, yet he has none of Job's anguished perplexity. That is because Kohelet, to all appearances, never had Job's experience of the goodness of God, with which the anarchy in the world might clash. Job might well have turned cynical had he never "heard" God in his earlier days.*

enmity, with their ultimate meaning clouded in mystery, than to accept a cold-blooded toying with the fortunes and lives of men.

Nonetheless, the Framework story says that one reason for senseless suffering is to test the motives of a pious man. This is stated only as the particular circumstance of this case and not as a general principle: one pious man, famous for his integrity, was visited with calamity for no reason other than to prove his character. That the same reason may apply to other pious men on whom senseless calamity falls is not said. But it is a possibility, one which lends a potentially heroic dimension to every such case; that is the exemplary value of the book.

Job ends up a wiser man, for he sees better the nature of God's work in the world and recognizes the limitations of his former viewpoint. The manifestation of his peace with God, of his renewed spiritual vigor, is that he reconstitutes his life. He is a vessel into which blessings can be poured; he who wished to have died at birth now fathers new sons and daughters. That, in addition to answering the demands of simple justice, is the significance of the Epilogue (which many critics have belittled as crass).

This concept of God contradicts not only that of the Wisdom of the Proverbs (in which the principle of just individual retribution is iterated in its simplest form) but that of the Torah and the Prophets as well. These writings bear the imprint of God's saving acts, the Exodus and the Conquest; they represent God as the maintainer of the moral order, and interpret events in terms of reward and punishment. But the Torah and the Prophets refer to the nation more than to the individual, and in their time no situation arose in which that concept failed. On the national level, Israel could always be regarded as falling short of righteousness and integrity; there were always elements within it that could rightly be reproached as deserving of punishment and, under the principle of collective responsibility established by the public covenant, of tainting the people at large with their guilt.

The later inability to find an explanation for national destiny in the Torah and the Prophets is reflected, not in Job, but in the apocalyptic literature that arose in the Hellenistic period. There was no explanation in the tradition for the persecution by Antiochus IV, which singled out those loyal to God while leaving the apostates in peace. The faithful were reconciled to their suffering only because they saw it as the preordained prelude to an eventual spiritual domination of the world by the Saints of the Most

High (Dan. 7.27). Taking his cue from hints in the Suffering Servant passages of Isaiah (also a response to those perplexed by a topsy-turvy world in which the heathen prospered and the devotees of the Lord were humiliated), the apocalyptic visionary of Daniel perceived the suffering of the righteous as a necessary phase in a determined sequence of universal salvation. Thus he lent a significance to the reasonless suffering of his community which was outside the categories of ordinary justice.

Is the retention in the biblical canon of Proverbs alongside Job, or the Torah and the Prophets alongside the apocalypses of Daniel, just thoughtless conservatism?

The religious sensibility apparently absorbs or even affirms the contradictions embodied in these books. That may be because these contradictions are perceived to exist in reality. One can see in individual life as in collective life a moral causality (which the religious regard as divinely maintained; indeed, as a reflection of God's attributes): evil recoils upon the evildoers, whether individual or collective; goodness brings blessings. At the same time, the manifestation of this causality can be so erratic or so delayed as to cast doubt on its validity as the single key to the destiny of men and nations. Hence the sober believer does not pin his faith solely on a simple axiom of the divine maintenance of moral causality, but neither will he altogether deny its force. No single key unlocks the mystery of destiny: "Within our ken is neither the tranquility of the wicked nor the suffering of the righteous" (Abot 4.17), but, for all that, the sober believer does not endorse nihilism. Wisdom, Torah, and Prophets continue to represent for him one aspect of causality in events which he can confirm in his own private experience. But one aspect only. The other stands beyond his moral judgment, though it is still under God: namely, the mysterious or preordained decree of God, toward which the proper attitude is "Though He slay me, yet will I trust in Him" (Job 13.15, *qere*).

ספר איוב THE BOOK OF JOB

א
1 אִישׁ הָיָה בְאֶרֶץ־עוּץ אִיּוֹב שְׁמוֹ
וְהָיָה ׀ הָאִישׁ הַהוּא תָּם וְיָשָׁר וִירֵא
2 אֱלֹהִים וְסָר מֵרָע׃ וַיִּוָּלְדוּ לוֹ שִׁבְעָה
3 בָנִים וְשָׁלוֹשׁ בָּנוֹת׃ וַיְהִי מִקְנֵהוּ
שִׁבְעַת אַלְפֵי־צֹאן וּשְׁלֹשֶׁת אַלְפֵי
גְמַלִּים וַחֲמֵשׁ מֵאוֹת צֶמֶד־בָּקָר
וַחֲמֵשׁ מֵאוֹת אֲתוֹנוֹת וַעֲבֻדָּה רַבָּה
מְאֹד וַיְהִי הָאִישׁ הַהוּא גָּדוֹל מִכָּל־
4 בְּנֵי־קֶדֶם׃ וְהָלְכוּ בָנָיו וְעָשׂוּ
מִשְׁתֶּה בֵּית אִישׁ יוֹמוֹ וְשָׁלְחוּ וְקָרְאוּ
לִשְׁלֹשֶׁת אַחְיֹתֵיהֶם לֶאֱכֹל וְלִשְׁתּוֹת
5 עִמָּהֶם׃ וַיְהִי כִּי הִקִּיפוּ יְמֵי הַמִּשְׁתֶּה
וַיִּשְׁלַח אִיּוֹב וַיְקַדְּשֵׁם וְהִשְׁכִּים בַּבֹּקֶר
וְהֶעֱלָה עֹלוֹת מִסְפַּר כֻּלָּם כִּי אָמַר
אִיּוֹב אוּלַי חָטְאוּ בָנַי וּבֵרֲכוּ אֱלֹהִים
בִּלְבָבָם כָּכָה יַעֲשֶׂה אִיּוֹב כָּל־
6 הַיָּמִים׃ וַיְהִי הַיּוֹם וַיָּבֹאוּ בְּנֵי
הָאֱלֹהִים לְהִתְיַצֵּב עַל־יְהוָה וַיָּבוֹא
7 גַם־הַשָּׂטָן בְּתוֹכָם׃ וַיֹּאמֶר יְהוָה
אֶל־הַשָּׂטָן מֵאַיִן תָּבֹא וַיַּעַן הַשָּׂטָן
אֶת־יְהוָה וַיֹּאמַר מִשּׁוּט בָּאָרֶץ
8 וּמֵהִתְהַלֵּךְ בָּהּ׃ וַיֹּאמֶר יְהוָה אֶל־
הַשָּׂטָן הֲשַׂמְתָּ לִבְּךָ עַל־עַבְדִּי אִיּוֹב
כִּי אֵין כָּמֹהוּ בָּאָרֶץ אִישׁ תָּם וְיָשָׁר
9 יְרֵא אֱלֹהִים וְסָר מֵרָע׃ וַיַּעַן הַשָּׂטָן
אֶת־יְהוָה וַיֹּאמַר הַחִנָּם יָרֵא אִיּוֹב
10 אֱלֹהִים׃ הֲלֹא־אַתְּ שַׂכְתָּ בַעֲדוֹ אתה ק׳
וּבְעַד־בֵּיתוֹ וּבְעַד כָּל־אֲשֶׁר־לוֹ
מִסָּבִיב מַעֲשֵׂה יָדָיו בֵּרַכְתָּ וּמִקְנֵהוּ
11 פָּרַץ בָּאָרֶץ׃ וְאוּלָם שְׁלַח־נָא יָדְךָ
וְגַע בְּכָל־אֲשֶׁר־לוֹ אִם־לֹא עַל־
12 פָּנֶיךָ יְבָרְכֶךָּ׃ וַיֹּאמֶר יְהוָה אֶל־
הַשָּׂטָן הִנֵּה כָל־אֲשֶׁר־לוֹ בְּיָדֶךָ רַק
אֵלָיו אַל־תִּשְׁלַח יָדֶךָ וַיֵּצֵא הַשָּׂטָן
13 מֵעִם פְּנֵי יְהוָה׃ וַיְהִי הַיּוֹם וּבָנָיו
וּבְנֹתָיו אֹכְלִים וְשֹׁתִים יַיִן בְּבֵית
14 אֲחִיהֶם הַבְּכוֹר׃ וּמַלְאָךְ בָּא אֶל־
אִיּוֹב וַיֹּאמַר הַבָּקָר הָיוּ חֹרְשׁוֹת
15 וְהָאֲתֹנוֹת רֹעוֹת עַל־יְדֵיהֶם׃ וַתִּפֹּל
שְׁבָא וַתִּקָּחֵם וְאֶת־הַנְּעָרִים הִכּוּ
לְפִי־חָרֶב וָאִמָּלְטָה רַק־אֲנִי

1 There was a man in the land of Uz named Job. That man was
blameless and upright; he feared God and shunned evil. 2 Seven
sons and three daughters were born to him; 3 his possessions
were seven thousand sheep, three thousand camels, five hundred
yoke of oxen and five hundred she-asses, and a very large household. That man was wealthier than anyone in the East.
4 It was the custom of his sons to hold feasts, each on his set
day in his own home. They would send word to their three sisters
to eat and drink with them. 5 When a round of feast days was over,
Job would send word to them to sanctify themselves, and, rising
early in the morning, he would make burnt offerings, one for
each of them; for Job thought, "Perhaps my children have sinned
and blasphemed God in their thoughts." This is what Job always
used to do.
6 One day the divine beings presented themselves before the
LORD,[a-]and the Adversary[-a] came along with them. 7 The LORD
said to the Adversary, "Where have you been?" The Adversary
answered the LORD, "I have been roaming all over the earth."
8 The LORD said to the Adversary, "Have you noticed My servant
Job? There is no one like him on earth, a blameless and upright
man who fears God and shuns evil!" 9 The Adversary answered
the LORD, "Does Job not have good reason to fear God? 10 Why,
it is You who have fenced him round, him and his household and
all that he has. You have blessed his efforts so that his possessions
spread out in the land. 11 But lay Your hand upon all that he has
and he will surely blaspheme You to Your face." 12 The LORD
replied to the Adversary, "See, all that he has is in your power;
only do not lay a hand on him." The Adversary departed from
the presence of the LORD.
13 One day, as his sons and daughters were eating and drinking
wine in the house of their eldest brother, 14 a messenger came to
Job and said, "The oxen were plowing and the asses were grazing
alongside them 15 when Sabeans attacked them and carried them
off, and put the boys to the sword; I alone have escaped to tell

a-a *Heb.* ha-saṭan.

לְבַדִּ֖י לְהַגִּ֥יד לָֽךְ׃ ע֤וֹד ׀ זֶ֣ה מְדַבֵּ֔ר ¹⁶
וְזֶ֗ה בָּ֚א וַיֹּאמַ֔ר אֵ֣שׁ אֱלֹהִ֗ים נָֽפְלָה֙
מִן־הַשָּׁמַ֔יִם וַתִּבְעַ֥ר בַּצֹּ֛אן וּבַנְּעָרִ֖ים
וַתֹּאכְלֵ֑ם וָאִמָּ֨לְטָ֧ה רַק־אֲנִ֛י לְבַדִּ֖י
לְהַגִּ֥יד לָֽךְ׃ ע֣וֹד ׀ זֶ֣ה מְדַבֵּ֗ר וְזֶה֮ בָּ֣א ¹⁷
וַיֹּאמַר֒ כַּשְׂדִּ֞ים שָׂמ֣וּ ׀ שְׁלֹשָׁ֣ה רָאשִׁ֗ים
וַֽיִּפְשְׁט֤וּ עַל־הַגְּמַלִּים֙ וַיִּקָּח֔וּם וְאֶת־
הַנְּעָרִ֖ים הִכּ֣וּ לְפִי־חָ֑רֶב וָאִמָּ֨לְטָ֧ה
רַק־אֲנִ֛י לְבַדִּ֖י לְהַגִּ֥יד לָֽךְ׃ עַ֣ד זֶ֣ה ¹⁸
מְדַבֵּ֔ר וְזֶ֖ה בָּ֣א וַיֹּאמַ֑ר בָּנֶ֨יךָ֙ וּבְנוֹתֶ֔יךָ
אֹֽכְלִ֥ים וְשֹׁתִ֛ים יַ֖יִן בְּבֵ֥ית אֲחִיהֶ֥ם
הַבְּכֽוֹר׃ וְהִנֵּה֩ ר֨וּחַ גְּדוֹלָ֜ה בָּ֣אָה ׀ ¹⁹
מֵעֵ֣בֶר הַמִּדְבָּ֗ר וַיִּגַּע֙ בְּאַרְבַּע֙ פִּנּ֣וֹת
הַבַּ֔יִת וַיִּפֹּ֥ל עַל־הַנְּעָרִ֖ים וַיָּמ֑וּתוּ
וָאִמָּ֨לְטָ֧ה רַק־אֲנִ֛י לְבַדִּ֖י לְהַגִּ֥יד לָֽךְ׃
וַיָּ֤קָם אִיּוֹב֙ וַיִּקְרַ֣ע אֶת־מְעִל֔וֹ וַיָּ֖גָז ²⁰
אֶת־רֹאשׁ֑וֹ וַיִּפֹּ֥ל אַ֖רְצָה וַיִּשְׁתָּֽחוּ׃
וַיֹּאמֶר֮ עָרֹ֣ם יָצָ֣אתִי מִבֶּ֣טֶן אִמִּי֒ וְעָרֹם֙ ²¹ חסר א
אָשׁ֣וּב שָׁ֔מָּה יְהֹוָ֣ה נָתַ֔ן וַיהֹוָ֖ה לָקָ֑ח
יְהִ֛י שֵׁ֥ם יְהֹוָ֖ה מְבֹרָֽךְ׃ בְּכׇל־זֹ֖את ²²
לֹא־חָטָ֣א אִיּ֑וֹב וְלֹא־נָתַ֥ן תִּפְלָ֖ה
לֵאלֹהִֽים׃

ב

וַיְהִ֣י הַיּ֔וֹם וַיָּבֹ֙אוּ֙ בְּנֵ֣י הָֽאֱלֹהִ֔ים ¹
לְהִתְיַצֵּ֖ב עַל־יְהֹוָ֑ה וַיָּב֥וֹא גַֽם־הַשָּׂטָ֛ן
בְּתֹכָ֖ם לְהִתְיַצֵּ֥ב עַל־יְהֹוָֽה׃ וַיֹּ֤אמֶר ²
יְהֹוָה֙ אֶל־הַשָּׂטָ֔ן אֵ֥י מִזֶּ֖ה תָּבֹ֑א וַיַּ֨עַן
הַשָּׂטָ֤ן אֶת־יְהֹוָה֙ וַיֹּאמַ֔ר מִשֻּׁ֥ט
בָּאָ֖רֶץ וּמֵהִתְהַלֵּ֥ךְ בָּֽהּ׃ וַיֹּ֤אמֶר יְהֹוָה֙ ³
אֶל־הַשָּׂטָ֔ן הֲשַׂ֥מְתָּ לִבְּךָ֖ אֶל־עַבְדִּ֣י
אִיּ֑וֹב כִּ֣י אֵ֤ין כָּמֹ֙הוּ֙ בָּאָ֔רֶץ אִ֣ישׁ תָּ֧ם
וְיָשָׁ֛ר יְרֵ֥א אֱלֹהִ֖ים וְסָ֣ר מֵרָ֑ע וְעֹדֶ֙נּוּ֙
מַחֲזִ֣יק בְּתֻמָּת֔וֹ וַתְּסִיתֵ֥נִי ב֖וֹ לְבַלְּע֥וֹ
חִנָּֽם׃ וַיַּ֧עַן הַשָּׂטָ֛ן אֶת־יְהֹוָ֖ה וַיֹּאמַ֑ר ⁴
ע֣וֹר בְּעַד־ע֗וֹר וְכֹל֙ אֲשֶׁ֣ר לָאִ֔ישׁ יִתֵּ֖ן
בְּעַ֥ד נַפְשֽׁוֹ׃ אוּלָם֙ שְֽׁלַֽח־נָ֣א יָֽדְךָ֔ ⁵
וְגַ֥ע אֶל־עַצְמ֖וֹ וְאֶל־בְּשָׂר֑וֹ אִם־
לֹ֥א אֶל־פָּנֶ֖יךָ יְבָרְכֶֽךָּ׃ וַיֹּ֧אמֶר יְהֹוָ֛ה ⁶
אֶל־הַשָּׂטָ֖ן הִנּ֣וֹ בְיָדֶ֑ךָ אַ֖ךְ אֶת־נַפְשׁ֥וֹ
שְׁמֹֽר׃ וַיֵּצֵא֙ הַשָּׂטָ֔ן מֵאֵ֖ת פְּנֵ֥י יְהֹוָ֑ה ⁷

you." ¹⁶ This one was still speaking when another came and said, "God's fire fell from heaven, took hold of the sheep and the boys, and burned them up; I alone have escaped to tell you." ¹⁷ This one was still speaking when another came and said, "A Chaldean formation of three columns made a raid on the camels and carried them off and put the boys to the sword; I alone have escaped to tell you." ¹⁸ This one was still speaking when another came and said, "Your sons and daughters were eating and drinking wine in the house of their eldest brother ¹⁹ when suddenly a mighty wind came from the wilderness. It struck the four corners of the house so that it collapsed upon the young people and they died; I alone have escaped to tell you."

²⁰ Then Job arose, tore his robe, cut off his hair, and threw himself on the ground and worshiped. ²¹ He said, "Naked came I out of my mother's womb, and naked shall I return there; the LORD has given, and the LORD has taken away; blessed be the name of the LORD."

²² For all that, Job did not sin nor did he cast reproach on God.

2 One day the divine beings presented themselves before the LORD. The Adversary came along with them to present himself before the LORD. ² The LORD said to the Adversary, "Where have you been?" The Adversary answered the LORD, "I have been roaming all over the earth." ³ The LORD said to the Adversary, "Have you noticed My servant Job? There is no one like him on earth, a blameless and upright man who fears God and shuns evil. He still keeps his integrity; so you have incited Me against him to destroy him for no good reason." ⁴ The Adversary answered the LORD, *a*-"Skin for skin-*a*—all that a man has he will give up for his life. ⁵ But lay a hand on his bones and his flesh, and he will surely blaspheme You to Your face." ⁶ So the LORD said to the Adversary, "See, he is in your power; only spare his life." ⁷ The Adversary departed from the presence of the LORD and inflicted

ᵃ⁻ᵃ *Apparently a proverb whose meaning is uncertain.*

וַיַּךְ אֶת־אִיּוֹב בִּשְׁחִין רָע מִכַּף רַגְלוֹ
8 עַד קָדְקֳדוֹ׃ וַיִּקַּח־לוֹ חֶרֶשׂ ועד ק׳
לְהִתְגָּרֵד בּוֹ וְהוּא יֹשֵׁב בְּתוֹךְ־
9 הָאֵפֶר׃ וַתֹּאמֶר לוֹ אִשְׁתּוֹ עֹדְךָ
מַחֲזִיק בְּתֻמָּתֶךָ בָּרֵךְ אֱלֹהִים וָמֻת׃
10 וַיֹּאמֶר אֵלֶיהָ כְּדַבֵּר אַחַת הַנְּבָלוֹת
תְּדַבֵּרִי גַּם אֶת־הַטּוֹב נְקַבֵּל מֵאֵת
הָאֱלֹהִים וְאֶת־הָרָע לֹא נְקַבֵּל
בְּכָל־זֹאת לֹא־חָטָא אִיּוֹב בִּשְׂפָתָיו׃
11 וַיִּשְׁמְעוּ שְׁלֹשֶׁת ׀ רֵעֵי אִיּוֹב אֵת כָּל־
הָרָעָה הַזֹּאת הַבָּאָה עָלָיו וַיָּבֹאוּ
אִישׁ מִמְּקֹמוֹ אֱלִיפַז הַתֵּימָנִי וּבִלְדַּד
הַשּׁוּחִי וְצוֹפַר הַנַּעֲמָתִי וַיִּוָּעֲדוּ יַחְדָּו
12 לָבוֹא לָנוּד־לוֹ וּלְנַחֲמוֹ׃ וַיִּשְׂאוּ אֶת־
עֵינֵיהֶם מֵרָחוֹק וְלֹא הִכִּירֻהוּ וַיִּשְׂאוּ
קוֹלָם וַיִּבְכּוּ וַיִּקְרְעוּ אִישׁ מְעִלוֹ
וַיִּזְרְקוּ עָפָר עַל־רָאשֵׁיהֶם
13 הַשָּׁמָיְמָה׃ וַיֵּשְׁבוּ אִתּוֹ לָאָרֶץ שִׁבְעַת
יָמִים וְשִׁבְעַת לֵילוֹת וְאֵין־דֹּבֵר אֵלָיו
דָּבָר כִּי רָאוּ כִּי־גָדַל הַכְּאֵב מְאֹד׃

a severe inflammation on Job from the sole of his foot to the
crown of his head. 8 He took a potsherd to scratch himself as he
sat in ashes. 9 His wife said to him, "You still keep your integrity!
Blaspheme God and die!" 10 But he said to her, "You talk as any
shameless woman might talk! Should we accept only good from
God and not accept evil?" For all that, Job said nothing sinful.

11 When Job's three friends heard about all these calamities
that had befallen him, each came from his home—Eliphaz the
Temanite, Bildad the Shuhite, and Zophar the Naamathite. They
met together to go and console and comfort him. 12 When they
saw him from a distance, they could not recognize him, and they
broke into loud weeping; each one tore his robe and threw dust
into the air onto his head. 13 They sat with him on the ground
seven days and seven nights. None spoke a word to him for they
saw how very great was his suffering.

ג

1 אַחֲרֵי־כֵן פָּתַח אִיּוֹב אֶת־פִּיהוּ
2 וַיְקַלֵּל אֶת־יוֹמוֹ׃ וַיַּעַן אִיּוֹב וַיֹּאמַר׃

3 יֹאבַד יוֹם אִוָּלֶד בּוֹ
וְהַלַּיְלָה אָמַר הֹרָה גָבֶר׃

4 הַיּוֹם הַהוּא יְהִי־חֹשֶׁךְ
אַל־יִדְרְשֵׁהוּ אֱלוֹהַּ מִמָּעַל פתח באתנח
וְאַל־תּוֹפַע עָלָיו נְהָרָה׃
5 יִגְאָלֻהוּ חֹשֶׁךְ וְצַלְמָוֶת
תִּשְׁכָּן־עָלָיו עֲנָנָה
יְבַעֲתֻהוּ כִּמְרִירֵי יוֹם׃
6 הַלַּיְלָה הַהוּא יִקָּחֵהוּ אֹפֶל
אַל־יִחַדְּ בִּימֵי שָׁנָה
בְּמִסְפַּר יְרָחִים אַל־יָבֹא׃
7 הִנֵּה הַלַּיְלָה הַהוּא יְהִי גַלְמוּד

3

[a]Afterward, Job began to speak and cursed the day of his
birth. 2 Job spoke up and said:

3 Perish the day on which I was born,
And the night it was announced,
"A male has been conceived!"
4 May that day be darkness;
May God above have no concern for it;
May light not shine on it;
5 May darkness and deep gloom look after it;
May a pall lie over it;
May [b]what blackens[b] the day terrify it.
6 May obscurity carry off that night;
May it not be counted among the days of the year;
May it not appear in any of its months;
7 May that night be desolate;

[a] *There are many difficulties in the poetry of Job, making the interpretation of words, verses, and even chapters uncertain. The rubric "Meaning of Heb. uncertain" in this book indicates only some of the extreme instances.*

[b-b] *Meaning of Heb. uncertain.*

אַל־תָּבוֹא רְנָנָה בוֹ׃
8 יִקְּבֻהוּ אֹרְרֵי־יוֹם
הָעֲתִידִים עֹרֵר לִוְיָתָן׃
9 יֶחְשְׁכוּ כּוֹכְבֵי נִשְׁפּוֹ
יְקַו־לְאוֹר וָאַיִן פתח באתנח
וְאַל־יִרְאֶה בְּעַפְעַפֵּי־שָׁחַר׃
10 כִּי לֹא סָגַר דַּלְתֵי בִטְנִי
וַיַּסְתֵּר עָמָל מֵעֵינָי׃
11 לָמָּה לֹּא מֵרֶחֶם אָמוּת
מִבֶּטֶן יָצָאתִי וְאֶגְוָע׃
12 מַדּוּעַ קִדְּמוּנִי בִרְכָּיִם
וּמַה־שָּׁדַיִם כִּי אִינָק׃
13 כִּי־עַתָּה שָׁכַבְתִּי וְאֶשְׁקוֹט
יָשַׁנְתִּי אָז ׀ יָנוּחַ לִי׃
14 עִם־מְלָכִים וְיֹעֲצֵי אָרֶץ
הַבֹּנִים חֳרָבוֹת לָמוֹ׃
15 אוֹ עִם־שָׂרִים זָהָב לָהֶם
הַמְמַלְאִים בָּתֵּיהֶם כָּסֶף׃
16 אוֹ כְנֵפֶל טָמוּן לֹא אֶהְיֶה
כְּעֹלְלִים לֹא־רָאוּ אוֹר׃
17 שָׁם רְשָׁעִים חָדְלוּ רֹגֶז
וְשָׁם יָנוּחוּ יְגִיעֵי כֹחַ׃
18 יַחַד אֲסִירִים שַׁאֲנָנוּ
לֹא שָׁמְעוּ קוֹל נֹגֵשׂ׃
19 קָטֹן וְגָדוֹל שָׁם הוּא
וְעֶבֶד חָפְשִׁי מֵאֲדֹנָיו׃

20 לָמָּה יִתֵּן לְעָמֵל אוֹר
וְחַיִּים לְמָרֵי נָפֶשׁ׃
21 הַמְחַכִּים לַמָּוֶת וְאֵינֶנּוּ
וַיַּחְפְּרֻהוּ מִמַּטְמוֹנִים׃
22 הַשְּׂמֵחִים אֱלֵי־גִיל
יָשִׂישׂוּ כִּי יִמְצְאוּ־קָבֶר׃
23 לְגֶבֶר אֲשֶׁר־דַּרְכּוֹ נִסְתָּרָה
וַיָּסֶךְ אֱלוֹהַּ בַּעֲדוֹ׃

24 כִּי־לִפְנֵי לַחְמִי אַנְחָתִי תָבֹא
וַיִּתְּכוּ כַמַּיִם שַׁאֲגֹתָי׃
25 כִּי פַחַד פָּחַדְתִּי וַיֶּאֱתָיֵנִי
וַאֲשֶׁר יָגֹרְתִּי יָבֹא לִי׃

May no sound of joy be heard in it;
8 May those who cast spells upon the day[c] damn it,
Those prepared to disable Leviathan;
9 May its twilight stars remain dark;
May it hope for light and have none;
May it not see the glimmerings of the dawn—
10 Because it did not block my mother's womb,
And hide trouble from my eyes.

11 Why did I not die at birth,
Expire as I came forth from the womb?
12 Why were there knees to receive me,
Or breasts for me to suck?
13 For now would I be lying in repose, asleep and at rest,
14 With the world's kings and counselors who rebuild ruins for themselves,
15 Or with nobles who possess gold and who fill their houses with silver.
16 Or why was I not like a buried stillbirth,
Like babies who never saw the light?
17 There the wicked cease from troubling;
There rest those whose strength is spent.
18 Prisoners are wholly at ease;
They do not hear the taskmaster's voice.
19 Small and great alike are there,
And the slave is free of his master.

20 Why does He give light to the sufferer
And life to the bitter in spirit;
21 To those who wait for death but it does not come,
Who search for it more than for treasure,
22 Who rejoice to exultation,
And are glad to reach the grave;
23 To the man who has lost his way,
Whom God has hedged about?

24 My groaning serves as my bread;
My roaring pours forth as water.
25 For what I feared has overtaken me;
What I dreaded has come upon me.

[c] *Or "sea," taking Heb.* yom *as equivalent of* yam; *compare the combination of sea with Leviathan in Ps. 74.13, 14 and with Dragon in Job 7.12; cf. also Isa. 27.1.*

26 לֹא שָׁלַוְתִּי ׀ וְלֹא־שָׁקַטְתִּי
וְלֹא־נָחְתִּי וַיָּבֹא רֹגֶז׃

26 I had no repose, no quiet, no rest,
And trouble came.

ד

1 וַיַּעַן אֱלִיפַז הַתֵּימָנִי וַיֹּאמַר׃

4

Then Eliphaz the Temanite said in reply:

2 הֲנִסָּה דָבָר אֵלֶיךָ תִּלְאֶה
וַעְצֹר בְּמִלִּין מִי יוּכָל׃
3 הִנֵּה יִסַּרְתָּ רַבִּים
וְיָדַיִם רָפוֹת תְּחַזֵּק׃
4 כּוֹשֵׁל יְקִימוּן מִלֶּיךָ
וּבִרְכַּיִם כֹּרְעוֹת תְּאַמֵּץ׃
5 כִּי עַתָּה ׀ תָּבוֹא אֵלֶיךָ וַתֵּלֶא
תִּגַּע עָדֶיךָ וַתִּבָּהֵל׃
6 הֲלֹא יִרְאָתְךָ כִּסְלָתֶךָ
תִּקְוָתְךָ וְתֹם דְּרָכֶיךָ׃
7 זְכָר־נָא מִי הוּא נָקִי אָבָד
וְאֵיפֹה יְשָׁרִים נִכְחָדוּ׃
8 כַּאֲשֶׁר רָאִיתִי חֹרְשֵׁי אָוֶן
וְזֹרְעֵי עָמָל יִקְצְרֻהוּ׃
9 מִנִּשְׁמַת אֱלוֹהַּ יֹאבֵדוּ
וּמֵרוּחַ אַפּוֹ יִכְלוּ׃
10 שַׁאֲגַת אַרְיֵה וְקוֹל שָׁחַל
וְשִׁנֵּי כְפִירִים נִתָּעוּ׃
11 לַיִשׁ אֹבֵד מִבְּלִי־טָרֶף
וּבְנֵי לָבִיא יִתְפָּרָדוּ׃

2 If one ventures a word with you, will it be too much?
But who can hold back his words?
3 See, you have encouraged many;
You have strengthened failing hands.
4 Your words have kept him who stumbled from falling;
You have braced knees that gave way.
5 But now that it overtakes you, it is too much;
It reaches you, and you are unnerved.
6 Is not your piety your confidence,
Your integrity your hope?
7 Think now, what innocent man ever perished?
Where have the upright been destroyed?
8 As I have seen, those who plow evil
And sow mischief reap them.
9 They perish by a blast from God,
Are gone at the breath of His nostrils.
10 The lion may roar, the cub may howl,
But the teeth of the king of beasts [a]are broken.[a]
11 The lion perishes for lack of prey,
And its whelps are scattered.

12 וְאֵלַי דָּבָר יְגֻנָּב
וַתִּקַּח אָזְנִי שֵׁמֶץ מֶנְהוּ׃
13 בִּשְׂעִפִּים מֵחֶזְיֹנוֹת לָיְלָה
בִּנְפֹל תַּרְדֵּמָה עַל־אֲנָשִׁים׃
14 פַּחַד קְרָאַנִי וּרְעָדָה
וְרֹב עַצְמוֹתַי הִפְחִיד׃
15 וְרוּחַ עַל־פָּנַי יַחֲלֹף
תְּסַמֵּר שַׂעֲרַת בְּשָׂרִי׃
16 יַעֲמֹד ׀ וְלֹא־אַכִּיר מַרְאֵהוּ
תְּמוּנָה לְנֶגֶד עֵינָי
דְּמָמָה וָקוֹל אֶשְׁמָע׃
17 הַאֱנוֹשׁ מֵאֱלוֹהַּ יִצְדָּק
אִם־מֵעֹשֵׂהוּ יִטְהַר גָּבֶר׃
18 הֵן בַּעֲבָדָיו לֹא יַאֲמִין

12 A word came to me in stealth;
My ear caught a whisper of it.
13 In thought-filled visions of the night,
When deep sleep falls on men,
14 Fear and trembling came upon me,
Causing all my bones to quake with fright.
15 A wind passed by me,
Making the hair of my flesh bristle.
16 It halted; its appearance was strange to me;
A form loomed before my eyes;
I heard a murmur, a voice,
17 "Can mortals be acquitted by God?
Can man be cleared by his Maker?
18 If He cannot trust His own servants,

a-a *Meaning of Heb. uncertain.*

וּבְמַלְאָכָיו יָשִׂים תָּהֳלָה׃
19 אַף ׀ שֹׁכְנֵי בָתֵּי־חֹמֶר
אֲשֶׁר־בֶּעָפָר יְסוֹדָם
יְדַכְּאוּם לִפְנֵי־עָשׁ׃
20 מִבֹּקֶר לָעֶרֶב יֻכַּתּוּ פתח באתנח
מִבְּלִי מֵשִׂים לָנֶצַח יֹאבֵדוּ׃
21 הֲלֹא־נִסַּע יִתְרָם בָּם
יָמוּתוּ וְלֹא בְחָכְמָה׃

And casts reproach[a] on His angels,
19 How much less those who dwell in houses of clay,
Whose origin is dust,
Who are crushed like the moth,
20 Shattered between daybreak and evening,
Perishing forever, unnoticed.
21 Their cord is pulled up
And they die, and not with wisdom."

ה
5

1 קְרָא־נָא הֲיֵשׁ עוֹנֶךָּ
וְאֶל־מִי מִקְּדֹשִׁים תִּפְנֶה׃
2 כִּי־לֶאֱוִיל יַהֲרָג־כָּעַשׂ
וּפֹתֶה תָּמִית קִנְאָה׃
3 אֲנִי־רָאִיתִי אֱוִיל מַשְׁרִישׁ
וָאֶקּוֹב נָוֵהוּ פִתְאֹם׃
4 יִרְחֲקוּ בָנָיו מִיֶּשַׁע
וְיִדַּכְּאוּ בַשַּׁעַר וְאֵין מַצִּיל׃

1 Call now! Will anyone answer you?
To whom among the holy beings will you turn?
2 Vexation kills the fool;
Passion slays the simpleton.
3 I myself saw a fool who had struck roots;
Impulsively, I cursed his home:
4 May his children be far from success;
May they be oppressed in the gate with none to deliver them;

5 אֲשֶׁר קְצִירוֹ ׀ רָעֵב יֹאכֵל
וְאֶל־מִצִּנִּים יִקָּחֵהוּ
וְשָׁאַף צַמִּים חֵילָם׃
6 כִּי ׀ לֹא־יֵצֵא מֵעָפָר אָוֶן
וּמֵאֲדָמָה לֹא־יִצְמַח עָמָל׃
7 כִּי־אָדָם לְעָמָל יוּלָּד דגש אחר שורק
וּבְנֵי־רֶשֶׁף יַגְבִּיהוּ עוּף׃

5 May the hungry devour his harvest,
[a]Carrying it off in baskets;
May the thirsty swallow their wealth.[a]
6 Evil does not grow out of the soil,
Nor does mischief spring from the ground;
7 For man is born for mischief,
Just as sparks fly upward.

8 אוּלָם אֲנִי אֶדְרֹשׁ אֶל־אֵל
וְאֶל־אֱלֹהִים אָשִׂים דִּבְרָתִי׃
9 עֹשֶׂה גְדֹלוֹת וְאֵין חֵקֶר
נִפְלָאוֹת עַד־אֵין מִסְפָּר׃
10 הַנֹּתֵן מָטָר עַל־פְּנֵי־אָרֶץ
וְשֹׁלֵחַ מַיִם עַל־פְּנֵי חוּצוֹת׃
11 לָשׂוּם שְׁפָלִים לְמָרוֹם
וְקֹדְרִים שָׂגְבוּ יֶשַׁע׃
12 מֵפֵר מַחְשְׁבוֹת עֲרוּמִים
וְלֹא־תַעֲשֶׂינָה יְדֵיהֶם תּוּשִׁיָּה׃
13 לֹכֵד חֲכָמִים בְּעָרְמָם
וַעֲצַת נִפְתָּלִים נִמְהָרָה׃
14 יוֹמָם יְפַגְּשׁוּ־חֹשֶׁךְ
וְכַלַּיְלָה יְמַשְׁשׁוּ בַצָּהֳרָיִם׃

8 But I would resort to God;
I would lay my case before God,
9 Who performs great deeds which cannot be fathomed,
Wondrous things without number;
10 Who gives rain to the earth,
And sends water over the fields;
11 Who raises the lowly up high,
So that the dejected are secure in victory;
12 Who thwarts the designs of the crafty,
So that their hands cannot gain success;
13 Who traps the clever in their own wiles;
The plans of the crafty go awry.
14 By day they encounter darkness,
At noon they grope as in the night.

a-a *Meaning of Heb. uncertain.*

15 וַיֹּשַׁע מֵחֶרֶב מִפִּיהֶם
וּמִיַּד חָזָק אֶבְיוֹן׃
16 וַתְּהִי לַדַּל תִּקְוָה
וְעֹלָתָה קָפְצָה פִּיהָ׃

15 But He saves the needy from the sword of their mouth,
From the clutches of the strong.
16 So there is hope for the wretched;
The mouth of wrongdoing is stopped.

17 הִנֵּה אַשְׁרֵי אֱנוֹשׁ יוֹכִחֶנּוּ אֱלוֹהַּ
וּמוּסַר שַׁדַּי אַל־תִּמְאָס׃
18 כִּי הוּא יַכְאִיב וְיֶחְבָּשׁ
יִמְחַץ וְיָדָו תִּרְפֶּינָה׃ וידיו ק׳
19 בְּשֵׁשׁ צָרוֹת יַצִּילֶךָּ
וּבְשֶׁבַע ׀ לֹא־יִגַּע בְּךָ רָע׃
20 בְּרָעָב פָּדְךָ מִמָּוֶת
וּבְמִלְחָמָה מִידֵי חָרֶב׃
21 בְּשׁוֹט לָשׁוֹן תֵּחָבֵא
וְלֹא־תִירָא מִשֹּׁד כִּי יָבוֹא׃
22 לְשֹׁד וּלְכָפָן תִּשְׂחָק
וּמֵחַיַּת הָאָרֶץ אַל־תִּירָא׃
23 כִּי עִם־אַבְנֵי הַשָּׂדֶה בְרִיתֶךָ
וְחַיַּת הַשָּׂדֶה הָשְׁלְמָה־לָךְ׃
24 וְיָדַעְתָּ כִּי־שָׁלוֹם אָהֳלֶךָ
וּפָקַדְתָּ נָוְךָ וְלֹא תֶחֱטָא׃
25 וְיָדַעְתָּ כִּי־רַב זַרְעֶךָ
וְצֶאֱצָאֶיךָ כְּעֵשֶׂב הָאָרֶץ׃
26 תָּבוֹא בְכֶלַח אֱלֵי־קָבֶר
כַּעֲלוֹת גָּדִישׁ בְּעִתּוֹ׃
27 הִנֵּה־זֹאת חֲקַרְנוּהָ כֶּן־הִיא
שְׁמָעֶנָּה וְאַתָּה דַע־לָךְ׃

17 See how happy is the man whom God reproves;
Do not reject the discipline of the Almighty.
18 He injures, but He binds up;
He wounds, but His hands heal.
19 He will deliver you from six troubles;
In seven no harm will reach you:
20 In famine He will redeem you from death,
In war, from the sword.
21 You will be sheltered from the scourging tongue;
You will have no fear when violence comes.
22 You will laugh at violence and starvation,
And have no fear of wild beasts.
23 For you will have a pact with the rocks in the field,
And the beasts of the field will be your allies.
24 You will know that all is well in your tent;
When you visit your wife[b] you will never fail.
25 You will see that your offspring are many,
Your descendants like the grass of the earth.
26 You will come to the grave [a]in ripe old age,[a]
As shocks of grain are taken away in their season.
27 See, we have inquired into this and it is so;
Accept it and make it your own.

ו
1 וַיַּעַן אִיּוֹב וַיֹּאמַר׃

6

1 Then Job said in reply:

2 לוּ שָׁקוֹל יִשָּׁקֵל כַּעְשִׂי
וְהַיָּתִי בְּמֹאזְנַיִם יִשְׂאוּ־יָחַד׃ והותי ק׳
3 כִּי־עַתָּה מֵחוֹל יַמִּים יִכְבָּד
עַל־כֵּן דְּבָרַי לָעוּ׃
4 כִּי חִצֵּי שַׁדַּי עִמָּדִי
אֲשֶׁר חֲמָתָם שֹׁתָה רוּחִי
בִּעוּתֵי אֱלוֹהַּ יַעַרְכוּנִי׃
5 הֲיִנְהַק־פֶּרֶא עֲלֵי־דֶשֶׁא
אִם יִגְעֶה־שּׁוֹר עַל־בְּלִילוֹ׃

2 If my anguish were weighed,
My full calamity laid on the scales,
3 It would be heavier than the sand of the sea;
That is why I spoke recklessly.[a]
4 For the arrows of the Almighty are in me;
My spirit absorbs their poison;
God's terrors are arrayed against me.
5 Does a wild ass bray when he has grass?
Does a bull bellow over his fodder?

[b] *Lit. "home."*

[a] *Meaning of Heb. uncertain.*

6 הֲיֵאָכֵל תָּפֵל מִבְּלִי־מֶלַח
אִם־יֶשׁ־טַעַם בְּרִיר חַלָּמוּת׃
7 מֵאֲנָה לִנְגּוֹעַ נַפְשִׁי
הֵמָּה כִּדְוֵי לַחְמִי׃

8 מִי־יִתֵּן תָּבוֹא שֶׁאֱלָתִי
וְתִקְוָתִי יִתֵּן אֱלוֹהַּ׃
9 וְיֹאֵל אֱלוֹהַּ וִידַכְּאֵנִי
יַתֵּר יָדוֹ וִיבַצְּעֵנִי׃
10 וּתְהִי־עוֹד ׀ נֶחָמָתִי
וַאֲסַלְּדָה בְחִילָה לֹא יַחְמוֹל
כִּי־לֹא כִחַדְתִּי אִמְרֵי קָדוֹשׁ׃
11 מַה־כֹּחִי כִּי אֲיַחֵל
וּמַה־קִּצִּי כִּי־אַאֲרִיךְ נַפְשִׁי׃
12 אִם־כֹּחַ אֲבָנִים כֹּחִי
אִם־בְּשָׂרִי נָחוּשׁ׃
13 הַאִם אֵין עֶזְרָתִי בִי
וְתֻשִׁיָּה נִדְּחָה מִמֶּנִּי׃

14 לַמָּס מֵרֵעֵהוּ חָסֶד
וְיִרְאַת שַׁדַּי יַעֲזוֹב׃
15 אַחַי בָּגְדוּ כְמוֹ־נָחַל
כַּאֲפִיק נְחָלִים יַעֲבֹרוּ׃
16 הַקֹּדְרִים מִנִּי־קָרַח
עָלֵימוֹ יִתְעַלֶּם־שָׁלֶג׃
17 בְּעֵת יְזֹרְבוּ נִצְמָתוּ
בְּחֻמּוֹ נִדְעֲכוּ מִמְּקוֹמָם׃
18 יִלָּפְתוּ אָרְחוֹת דַּרְכָּם
יַעֲלוּ בַתֹּהוּ וְיֹאבֵדוּ׃
19 הִבִּיטוּ אָרְחוֹת תֵּמָא
הֲלִיכֹת שְׁבָא קִוּוּ־לָמוֹ׃
20 בֹּשׁוּ כִּי־בָטָח
בָּאוּ עָדֶיהָ וַיֶּחְפָּרוּ׃
21 כִּי־עַתָּה הֱיִיתֶם לוֹ בנ״א לא כתיב לו ק׳
תִּרְאוּ חֲתַת וַתִּירָאוּ׃
22 הֲכִי־אָמַרְתִּי הָבוּ לִי
וּמִכֹּחֲכֶם שִׁחֲדוּ בַעֲדִי׃
23 וּמַלְּטוּנִי מִיַּד־צָר
וּמִיַּד עָרִיצִים תִּפְדּוּנִי׃
24 הוֹרוּנִי וַאֲנִי אַחֲרִישׁ

6 Can what is tasteless be eaten without salt?
Does [a-]mallow juice[-a] have any flavor?
7 I refuse to touch them;
They are like food when I am sick.

8 Would that my request were granted,
That God gave me what I wished for;
9 Would that God consented to crush me,
Loosed His hand and cut me off.
10 Then this would be my consolation,
[a-]As I writhed in unsparing[-a] pains:
That I did not [b-]suppress my words against the Holy One.[-b]
11 What strength have I, that I should hope?
How long have I to live, that I should be patient?
12 Is my strength the strength of rock?
Is my flesh bronze?
13 Truly, I cannot help myself;
I have been deprived of resourcefulness.

14 [a-]A friend owes loyalty to one who fails,
Though he forsakes the fear of the Almighty;[-a]
15 My comrades are fickle, like a wadi,
Like a bed on which streams once ran.
16 [a-]They are dark with ice;
Snow obscures them;[-a]
17 But when they thaw, they vanish;
In the heat, they disappear where they are.
18 Their course twists and turns;
They run into the desert and perish.
19 Caravans from Tema look to them;
Processions from Sheba count on them.
20 They are disappointed in their hopes;
When they reach the place, they stand aghast.
21 So you are as nothing:[c]
At the sight of misfortune, you take fright.
22 Did I say to you, "I need your gift;
Pay a bribe for me out of your wealth;
23 Deliver me from the clutches of my enemy;
Redeem me from violent men"?
24 Teach me; I shall be silent;

[b-b] *Meaning of Heb. uncertain; others, "deny the words of the Holy One."*
[c] *Following* kethib, *with Targum; meaning of Heb. uncertain.*

וּמַה־שָּׁגִיתִי הָבִינוּ לִי׃
25 מַה־נִּמְרְצוּ אִמְרֵי־יֹשֶׁר
וּמַה־יּוֹכִיחַ הוֹכֵחַ מִכֶּם׃
26 הַלְהוֹכַח מִלִּים תַּחְשֹׁבוּ
וּלְרוּחַ אִמְרֵי נֹאָשׁ׃
27 אַף עַל־יָתוֹם תַּפִּילוּ
וְתִכְרוּ עַל־רֵיעֲכֶם׃
28 וְעַתָּה הוֹאִילוּ פְנוּ־בִי
וְעַל־פְּנֵיכֶם אִם־אֲכַזֵּב׃
29 שֻׁבוּ נָא אַל־תְּהִי עַוְלָה
וְשֻׁבִי עוֹד צִדְקִי־בָהּ׃ ושבו ק׳
30 הֲיֵשׁ־בִּלְשׁוֹנִי עַוְלָה
אִם־חִכִּי לֹא־יָבִין הַוּוֹת׃

ז
1 הֲלֹא־צָבָא לֶאֱנוֹשׁ עֲלֵ־אָרֶץ עלי ק׳
וְכִימֵי שָׂכִיר יָמָיו׃
2 כְּעֶבֶד יִשְׁאַף־צֵל
וּכְשָׂכִיר יְקַוֶּה פָעֳלוֹ׃
3 כֵּן הָנְחַלְתִּי לִי יַרְחֵי־שָׁוְא
וְלֵילוֹת עָמָל מִנּוּ־לִי׃
4 אִם־שָׁכַבְתִּי וְאָמַרְתִּי מָתַי אָקוּם
וּמִדַּד־עָרֶב
וְשָׂבַעְתִּי נְדֻדִים עֲדֵי־נָשֶׁף׃
5 לָבַשׁ בְּשָׂרִי רִמָּה וְגִישׁ עָפָר ג׳ זעירא וגוש ק׳
עוֹרִי רָגַע וַיִּמָּאֵס׃
6 יָמַי קַלּוּ מִנִּי־אָרֶג
וַיִּכְלוּ בְּאֶפֶס תִּקְוָה׃
7 זְכֹר כִּי־רוּחַ חַיָּי
לֹא־תָשׁוּב עֵינִי לִרְאוֹת טוֹב׃
8 לֹא־תְשׁוּרֵנִי עֵין רֹאִי
עֵינֶיךָ בִּי וְאֵינֶנִּי׃
9 כָּלָה עָנָן וַיֵּלַךְ פתח באתנח
כֵּן יוֹרֵד שְׁאוֹל לֹא יַעֲלֶה׃
10 לֹא־יָשׁוּב עוֹד לְבֵיתוֹ
וְלֹא־יַכִּירֶנּוּ עוֹד מְקוֹמוֹ׃

11 גַּם־אֲנִי לֹא אֶחֱשָׂךְ־פִּי
אֲדַבְּרָה בְּצַר רוּחִי

Tell me where I am wrong.
25 [a]How trenchant honest words are;[a]
But what sort of reproof comes from you?
26 Do you devise words of reproof,
But count a hopeless man's words as mere wind?
27 You would even cast lots over an orphan,
Or barter away your friend.
28 Now be so good as to face me;
I will not lie to your face.
29 Relent! Let there not be injustice;
Relent! I am still in the right.
30 Is injustice on my tongue?
Can my palate not discern evil?

7

Truly man has a term of service on earth;
His days are like those of a hireling—
2 Like a slave who longs for [evening's] shadows,
Like a hireling who waits for his wage.
3 So have I been allotted months of futility;
Nights of misery have been apportioned to me.
4 When I lie down, I think,
"When shall I rise?"
Night [a]drags on,[a]
And I am sated with tossings till morning twilight.
5 My flesh is covered with maggots and clods of earth;
My skin is broken and festering.
6 My days fly faster than a weaver's shuttle,
And come to their end [b]without hope.[b]
7 Consider that my life is but wind;
I shall never see happiness again.
8 The eye that gazes on me will not see me;
Your eye will seek me, but I shall be gone.
9 As a cloud fades away,
So whoever goes down to Sheol does not come up;
10 He returns no more to his home;
His place does not know him.

11 On my part, I will not speak with restraint;
I will give voice to the anguish of my spirit;

a-a *Meaning of Heb. uncertain.*
b-b *Or "when the thread runs out."*

אָשִׂיחָה בְּמַר נַפְשִׁי׃
12 הֲיָם־אָנִי אִם־תַּנִּין
כִּי־תָשִׂים עָלַי מִשְׁמָר׃
13 כִּי־אָמַרְתִּי תְּנַחֲמֵנִי עַרְשִׂי
יִשָּׂא בְשִׂיחִי מִשְׁכָּבִי׃
14 וְחִתַּתַּנִי בַחֲלֹמוֹת
וּמֵחֶזְיֹנוֹת תְּבַעֲתַנִּי׃ פתח בס״ף
15 וַתִּבְחַר מַחֲנָק נַפְשִׁי
מָוֶת מֵעַצְמוֹתָי׃
16 מָאַסְתִּי לֹא־לְעֹלָם אֶחְיֶה
חֲדַל מִמֶּנִּי כִּי־הֶבֶל יָמָי׃

I will complain in the bitterness of my soul.
12 Am I the sea or the Dragon,[c]
That You have set a watch over me?
13 When I think, "My bed will comfort me,
My couch will share my sorrow,"
14 You frighten me with dreams,
And terrify me with visions,
15 Till I prefer strangulation,
Death, to my wasted frame.
16 I am sick of it.
I shall not live forever;
Let me be, for my days are a breath.

17 מָה־אֱנוֹשׁ כִּי תְגַדְּלֶנּוּ
וְכִי־תָשִׁית אֵלָיו לִבֶּךָ׃
18 וַתִּפְקְדֶנּוּ לִבְקָרִים
לִרְגָעִים תִּבְחָנֶנּוּ׃
19 כַּמָּה לֹא־תִשְׁעֶה מִמֶּנִּי
לֹא תַרְפֵּנִי עַד־בִּלְעִי רֻקִּי׃
20 חָטָאתִי מָה אֶפְעַל ׀ לָךְ נֹצֵר הָאָדָם
לָמָה שַׂמְתַּנִי לְמִפְגָּע לָךְ רפי ומלעיל
וָאֶהְיֶה עָלַי לְמַשָּׂא׃

17 What is man, that You make much of him,
That You fix Your attention upon him?
18 You inspect him every morning,
Examine him every minute.
19 Will You not look away from me for a while,
Let me be, till I swallow my spittle?
20 If I have sinned, what have I done to You,
Watcher of men?
Why make of me Your target,
And a burden to myself?

21 וּמֶה ׀ לֹא־תִשָּׂא פִשְׁעִי
וְתַעֲבִיר אֶת־עֲוֺנִי
כִּי־עַתָּה לֶעָפָר אֶשְׁכָּב
וְשִׁחֲרְתַּנִי וְאֵינֶנִּי׃

21 Why do You not pardon my transgression
And forgive my iniquity?
For soon I shall lie down in the dust;
When You seek me, I shall be gone.

ח

8

1 וַיַּעַן בִּלְדַּד הַשּׁוּחִי וַיֹּאמַר׃

Bildad the Shuhite said in reply:

2 עַד־אָן תְּמַלֶּל־אֵלֶּה
וְרוּחַ כַּבִּיר אִמְרֵי־פִיךָ׃
3 הַאֵל יְעַוֵּת מִשְׁפָּט
וְאִם־שַׁדַּי יְעַוֵּת־צֶדֶק׃
4 אִם־בָּנֶיךָ חָטְאוּ־לוֹ
וַיְשַׁלְּחֵם בְּיַד־פִּשְׁעָם׃
5 אִם־אַתָּה תְּשַׁחֵר אֶל־אֵל
וְאֶל־שַׁדַּי תִּתְחַנָּן׃
6 אִם־זַךְ וְיָשָׁר אָתָּה
כִּי־עַתָּה יָעִיר עָלֶיךָ

2 How long will you speak such things?
Your utterances are a mighty wind!
3 Will God pervert the right?
Will the Almighty pervert justice?
4 If your sons sinned against Him,
He dispatched them for their transgression.
5 But if you seek God
And supplicate the Almighty,
6 If you are blameless and upright,
He will protect you,

[c] *See note at 3.8.*

וְשִׁלַּם נְוַת צִדְקֶךָ׃
7 וְהָיָה רֵאשִׁיתְךָ מִצְעָר
וְאַחֲרִיתְךָ יִשְׂגֶּה מְאֹד׃

8 כִּי־שְׁאַל־נָא לְדֹר רִישׁוֹן י׳ במקום א׳
וְכוֹנֵן לְחֵקֶר אֲבוֹתָם׃
9 כִּי־תְמוֹל אֲנַחְנוּ וְלֹא נֵדָע
כִּי צֵל יָמֵינוּ עֲלֵי־אָרֶץ׃
10 הֲלֹא־הֵם יוֹרוּךָ יֹאמְרוּ לָךְ
וּמִלִּבָּם יוֹצִאוּ מִלִּים׃
11 הֲיִגְאֶה־גֹּמֶא בְּלֹא בִצָּה
יִשְׂגֶּה־אָחוּ בְלִי־מָיִם׃
12 עֹדֶנּוּ בְאִבּוֹ לֹא יִקָּטֵף
וְלִפְנֵי כָל־חָצִיר יִיבָשׁ׃
13 כֵּן אָרְחוֹת כָּל־שֹׁכְחֵי אֵל
וְתִקְוַת חָנֵף תֹּאבֵד׃
14 אֲשֶׁר־יָקוֹט כִּסְלוֹ
וּבֵית עַכָּבִישׁ מִבְטַחוֹ׃
15 יִשָּׁעֵן עַל־בֵּיתוֹ וְלֹא יַעֲמֹד
יַחֲזִיק בּוֹ וְלֹא יָקוּם׃
16 רָטֹב הוּא לִפְנֵי־שָׁמֶשׁ
וְעַל־גַּנָּתוֹ יֹנַקְתּוֹ תֵצֵא׃
17 עַל־גַּל שָׁרָשָׁיו יְסֻבָּכוּ
בֵּית אֲבָנִים יֶחֱזֶה׃
18 אִם־יְבַלְּעֶנּוּ מִמְּקוֹמוֹ
וְכִחֶשׁ בּוֹ לֹא רְאִיתִיךָ׃

19 הֶן־הוּא מְשׂוֹשׂ דַּרְכּוֹ
וּמֵעָפָר אַחֵר יִצְמָחוּ׃
20 הֶן־אֵל לֹא יִמְאַס־תָּם
וְלֹא יַחֲזִיק בְּיַד־מְרֵעִים׃
21 עַד־יְמַלֵּה שְׂחוֹק פִּיךָ ה׳ במקום א׳
וּשְׂפָתֶיךָ תְרוּעָה׃
22 שֹׂנְאֶיךָ יִלְבְּשׁוּ־בֹשֶׁת
וְאֹהֶל רְשָׁעִים אֵינֶנּוּ׃

ט
1 וַיַּעַן אִיּוֹב וַיֹּאמַר׃

2 אָמְנָם יָדַעְתִּי כִי־כֵן
וּמַה־יִּצְדַּק אֱנוֹשׁ עִם־אֵל׃

And grant well-being to your righteous home.
7 Though your beginning be small,
In the end you will grow very great.

8 Ask the generation past,
Study what their fathers have searched out
9 —For we are of yesterday and know nothing;
Our days on earth are a shadow—
10 Surely they will teach you and tell you,
Speaking out of their understanding.
11 Can papyrus thrive without marsh?
Can rushes grow without water?
12 While still tender, not yet plucked,
They would wither quicker than any grass.
13 Such is the fate of all who forget God;
The hope of the impious man comes to naught—
14 Whose confidence is a [a]thread of gossamer,[a]
Whose trust is a spider's web.
15 He leans on his house—it will not stand;
He seizes hold of it, but it will not hold.
16 He stays fresh even in the sun;
His shoots spring up in his garden;
17 [a]His roots are twined around a heap,
They take hold of a house of stones.[a]
18 When he is uprooted from his place,
It denies him, [saying,]
"I never saw you."
19 Such is his happy lot;
And from the earth others will grow.
20 Surely God does not despise the blameless;
He gives no support to evildoers.
21 He will yet fill your mouth with laughter,
And your lips with shouts of joy.
22 Your enemies will be clothed in disgrace;
The tent of the wicked will vanish.

9

Job said in reply:

2 Indeed I know that it is so:
Man cannot win a suit against God.

a-a *Meaning of Heb. uncertain.*

3 אִם־יַחְפֹּץ לָרִיב עִמּוֹ
לֹא יַעֲנֶנּוּ אַחַת מִנִּי־אָלֶף׃
4 חֲכַם לֵבָב וְאַמִּיץ כֹּחַ
מִי־הִקְשָׁה אֵלָיו וַיִּשְׁלָם׃
5 הַמַּעְתִּיק הָרִים וְלֹא יָדָעוּ
אֲשֶׁר הֲפָכָם בְּאַפּוֹ׃
6 הַמַּרְגִּיז אֶרֶץ מִמְּקוֹמָהּ
וְעַמּוּדֶיהָ יִתְפַלָּצוּן׃
7 הָאֹמֵר לַחֶרֶס וְלֹא יִזְרָח
וּבְעַד כּוֹכָבִים יַחְתֹּם׃
8 נֹטֶה שָׁמַיִם לְבַדּוֹ
וְדוֹרֵךְ עַל־בָּמֳתֵי־יָם׃
9 עֹשֶׂה עָשׁ כְּסִיל
וְכִימָה וְחַדְרֵי תֵמָן׃
10 עֹשֶׂה גְדֹלוֹת עַד־אֵין חֵקֶר
וְנִפְלָאוֹת עַד־אֵין מִסְפָּר׃
11 הֵן יַעֲבֹר עָלַי וְלֹא אֶרְאֶה
וְיַחֲלֹף וְלֹא־אָבִין לוֹ׃
12 הֵן יַחְתֹּף מִי יְשִׁיבֶנּוּ
מִי־יֹאמַר אֵלָיו מַה־תַּעֲשֶׂה׃
13 אֱלוֹהַּ לֹא־יָשִׁיב אַפּוֹ
תַּחְתָּו שָׁחֲחוּ עֹזְרֵי רָהַב׃ תחתיו ק׳
14 אַף כִּי־אָנֹכִי אֶעֱנֶנּוּ
אֶבְחֲרָה דְבָרַי עִמּוֹ׃
15 אֲשֶׁר אִם־צָדַקְתִּי לֹא אֶעֱנֶה
לִמְשֹׁפְטִי אֶתְחַנָּן׃
16 אִם־קָרָאתִי וַיַּעֲנֵנִי
לֹא אַאֲמִין כִּי־יַאֲזִין קוֹלִי׃
17 אֲשֶׁר־בִּשְׂעָרָה יְשׁוּפֵנִי
וְהִרְבָּה פְצָעַי חִנָּם׃
18 לֹא־יִתְּנֵנִי הָשֵׁב רוּחִי
כִּי יַשְׂבִּעַנִי מַמְּרֹרִים׃
19 אִם־לְכֹחַ אַמִּיץ הִנֵּה
וְאִם־לְמִשְׁפָּט מִי יוֹעִידֵנִי׃
20 אִם־אֶצְדָּק פִּי יַרְשִׁיעֵנִי
תָּם אָנִי וַיַּעְקְשֵׁנִי׃
21 תָּם אָנִי לֹא־אֵדַע נַפְשִׁי
אֶמְאַס חַיָּי׃

3 If he insisted on a trial with Him,
He would not answer one charge in a thousand.
4 Wise of heart and mighty in power—
Who ever challenged Him and came out whole?—
5 Him who moves mountains without their knowing it,
Who overturns them in His anger;
6 Who shakes the earth from its place,
Till its pillars quake;
7 Who commands the sun not to shine;
Who seals up the stars;
8 Who by Himself spread out the heavens,
And trod on the back of the Sea;
9 Who made the Bear[a] and Orion,
Pleiades, and the chambers of the south wind;
10 Who performs great deeds which cannot be fathomed,
And wondrous things without number.
11 He passes me by—I do not see Him;
He goes by me, but I do not perceive Him.
12 He snatches away—who can stop Him?
Who can say to Him, "What are You doing?"
13 God does not restrain His anger;
Under Him Rahab's[b] helpers sink down.
14 How then can I answer Him,
Or choose my arguments against Him?
15 Though I were in the right, I could not speak out,
But I would plead for mercy with my judge.
16 If I summoned Him and He responded,
I do not believe He would lend me His ear.
17 For He crushes me [c]for a hair;[c]
He wounds me much for no cause.
18 He does not let me catch my breath,
But sates me with bitterness.
19 If a trial of strength—He is the strong one;
If a trial in court—who will summon Him for me?
20 Though I were innocent,
My mouth would condemn me;
Though I were blameless, He would prove me crooked.
21 I am blameless, yet I am distraught;
I am sick of life.

[a] *Meaning of Heb. uncertain.*
[b] *A primeval monster.*
[c-c] *With Targum and Peshitta; or "with a storm."*

²² אַחַת הִיא עַל־כֵּן אָמַ֒רְתִּי פתח באתנח

תָּם וְרָשָׁע ה֣וּא מְכַלֶּֽה׃

²³ אִם־שׁ֭וֹט יָמִ֣ית פִּתְאֹ֑ם

לְמַסַּ֖ת נְקִיִּ֣ם יִלְעָֽג׃

²⁴ אֶ֤רֶץ ׀ נִתְּנָ֬ה בְֽיַד־רָשָׁ֗ע

פְּנֵֽי־שֹׁפְטֶ֥יהָ יְכַסֶּ֑ה

אִם־לֹ֖א אֵפ֣וֹא מִי־הֽוּא׃

²⁵ וְיָמַ֣י קַ֭לּוּ מִנִּי־רָ֑ץ

בָּ֝רְח֗וּ לֹא־רָא֥וּ טוֹבָֽה׃

²⁶ חָ֭לְפוּ עִם־אֳנִיּ֣וֹת אֵבֶ֑ה

כְּ֝נֶ֗שֶׁר יָט֥וּשׂ עֲלֵי־אֹֽכֶל׃

²⁷ אִם־אׇ֭מְרִי אֶשְׁכְּחָ֣ה שִׂיחִ֑י

אֶעֶזְבָ֖ה פָנַ֣י וְאַבְלִֽיגָה׃

²⁸ יָגֹ֥רְתִּי כׇל־עַצְּבֹתָ֑י

יָ֝דַ֗עְתִּי כִּי־לֹ֥א תְנַקֵּֽנִי׃

²⁹ אָנֹכִ֥י אֶרְשָׁ֑ע

לָמָּה־זֶּ֝֗ה הֶ֣בֶל אִיגָֽע׃

³⁰ אִם־הִתְרָחַ֥צְתִּי בְמוֹ־שָׁ֑לֶג ב״נ י״ק

וַ֝הֲזִכּ֗וֹתִי בְּבֹ֣ר כַּפָּֽי׃ נ״א בבור

³¹ אָ֭ז בַּשַּׁ֣חַת תִּטְבְּלֵ֑נִי

וְ֝תִֽעֲב֗וּנִי שַׂלְמוֹתָֽי׃

³² כִּי־לֹא־אִ֣ישׁ כָּמ֣וֹנִי אֶֽעֱנֶ֑נּוּ

נָב֥וֹא יַ֝חְדָּ֗ו בַּמִּשְׁפָּֽט׃

³³ לֹ֣א יֵשׁ־בֵּינֵ֣ינוּ מוֹכִ֑יחַ

יָשֵׁ֖ת יָד֣וֹ עַל־שְׁנֵֽינוּ׃

³⁴ יָסֵ֣ר מֵעָלַ֣י שִׁבְט֑וֹ ט׳ רבתי

וְ֝אֵמָת֗וֹ אַֽל־תְּבַעֲתַֽנִּי׃ פתח בס״פ

³⁵ אֲֽדַבְּרָ֗ה וְלֹ֣א אִירָאֶ֑נּוּ

כִּ֥י לֹא־כֵ֥ן אָ֝נֹכִ֗י עִמָּדִֽי׃

10

¹ נׇקְטָ֥ה נַפְשִׁ֗י בְּחַ֫יָּ֥י

אֶעֶזְבָ֣ה עָלַ֣י שִׂיחִ֑י

אֲ֝דַבְּרָ֗ה בְּמַ֣ר נַפְשִֽׁי׃

² אֹמַ֣ר אֶל־אֱ֭לוֹהַּ אַל־תַּרְשִׁיעֵ֑נִי

ה֝וֹדִיעֵ֗נִי עַ֣ל מַה־תְּרִיבֵֽנִי׃

³ הֲט֤וֹב לְךָ֨ ׀ כִּֽי־תַעֲשֹׁ֗ק

כִּֽי־תִ֭מְאַס יְגִ֣יעַ כַּפֶּ֑יךָ

וְעַל־עֲצַ֖ת רְשָׁעִ֣ים הוֹפָֽעְתָּ׃

⁴ הַעֵינֵ֣י בָשָׂ֣ר לָ֑ךְ

²² It is all one. Therefore I say,
"He destroys the blameless and the guilty."
²³ When suddenly a scourge brings death,
He mocks as the innocent fail.
²⁴ The earth is handed over to the wicked one;
He covers the eyes of its judges.
If it is not He, then who?

²⁵ My days fly swifter than a runner;
They flee without seeing happiness;
²⁶ They pass like reed-boats,
Like an eagle swooping onto its prey.
²⁷ If I say, "I will forget my complaint;
Abandon my sorrow[d] and be diverted,"
²⁸ I remain in dread of all my suffering;
I know that You will not acquit me.
²⁹ It will be I who am in the wrong;
Why then should I waste effort?
³⁰ If I washed in soap,
Cleansed my hands with lye,
³¹ You would dip me in muck
Till my clothes would abhor me.
³² He is not a man, like me, that I can answer Him,
That we can go to law together.
³³ No arbiter is between us
To lay his hand on us both.
³⁴ If He would only take His rod away from me
And not let His terror frighten me,
³⁵ Then I would speak out without fear of Him;
For I know myself not to be so.

10 I am disgusted with life;
I will give rein to my complaint,
Speak in the bitterness of my soul.
² I say to God, "Do not condemn me;
Let me know with what You charge me.
³ Does it benefit You to defraud,
To despise the toil of Your hands,
While smiling on the counsel of the wicked?
⁴ Do You have the eyes of flesh?

---

d Lit. "face."

אִם־כִּרְאוֹת אֱנוֹשׁ תִּרְאֶה:	Is Your vision that of mere men?
5 הֲכִימֵי אֱנוֹשׁ יָמֶיךָ	5 Are Your days the days of a mortal,
אִם־שְׁנוֹתֶיךָ כִּימֵי גָבֶר:	Are Your years the years of a man,
6 כִּי־תְבַקֵּשׁ לַעֲוֺנִי	6 That You seek my iniquity
וּלְחַטָּאתִי תִדְרוֹשׁ:	And search out my sin?
7 עַל־דַּעְתְּךָ כִּי־לֹא אֶרְשָׁע	7 You know that I am not guilty,
וְאֵין מִיָּדְךָ מַצִּיל:	And that there is none to deliver from Your hand.
8 יָדֶיךָ עִצְּבוּנִי וַיַּעֲשׂוּנִי	8 "Your hands shaped and fashioned me,
יַחַד סָבִיב וַתְּבַלְּעֵנִי:	Then destroyed every part of me.
9 זְכָר־נָא כִּי־כַחֹמֶר עֲשִׂיתָנִי	9 Consider that You fashioned me as clay;
וְאֶל־עָפָר תְּשִׁיבֵנִי:	Will You then turn me back into dust?
10 הֲלֹא כֶחָלָב תַּתִּיכֵנִי	10 You poured me out like milk,
וְכַגְּבִנָּה תַּקְפִּיאֵנִי:	Congealed me like cheese;
11 עוֹר וּבָשָׂר תַּלְבִּישֵׁנִי	11 You clothed me with skin and flesh
וּבַעֲצָמוֹת וְגִידִים תְּשֹׂכְכֵנִי:	And wove me of bones and sinews;
12 חַיִּים וָחֶסֶד עָשִׂיתָ עִמָּדִי	12 You bestowed on me life and care;
וּפְקֻדָּתְךָ שָׁמְרָה רוּחִי:	Your providence watched over my spirit.
13 וְאֵלֶּה צָפַנְתָּ בִלְבָבֶךָ	13 Yet these things You hid in Your heart;
יָדַעְתִּי כִּי־זֹאת עִמָּךְ:	I know that You had this in mind:
14 אִם־חָטָאתִי וּשְׁמַרְתָּנִי	14 To watch me when I sinned
וּמֵעֲוֺנִי לֹא תְנַקֵּנִי:	And not clear me of my iniquity;
15 אִם־רָשַׁעְתִּי אַלְלַי לִי	15 Should I be guilty—the worse for me!
וְצָדַקְתִּי לֹא־אֶשָּׂא רֹאשִׁי	And even when innocent, I cannot lift my head;
שְׂבַע קָלוֹן וּרְאֵה עָנְיִי:	So sated am I with shame,
	And drenched in my misery.
16 וְיִגְאֶה כַּשַּׁחַל תְּצוּדֵנִי	16 [a]It is something to be proud of[a] to hunt me like a lion,
וְתָשֹׁב תִּתְפַּלָּא בִי:	To show Yourself wondrous through me time and again!
17 תְּחַדֵּשׁ עֵדֶיךָ ׀ נֶגְדִּי	17 You keep sending fresh witnesses against me,
וְתֶרֶב כַּעַשְׂךָ עִמָּדִי	Letting Your vexation with me grow.
חֲלִיפוֹת וְצָבָא עִמִּי:	[a]I serve my term and am my own replacement.[a]
18 וְלָמָּה מֵרֶחֶם הֹצֵאתָנִי	18 "Why did You let me come out of the womb?
אֶגְוַע וְעַיִן לֹא־תִרְאֵנִי:	Better had I expired before any eye saw me,
19 כַּאֲשֶׁר לֹא־הָיִיתִי אֶהְיֶה	19 Had I been as though I never was,
מִבֶּטֶן לַקֶּבֶר אוּבָל:	Had I been carried from the womb to the grave.
20 הֲלֹא־מְעַט יָמַי יֶחְדָּל — וחדל ק	20 My days are few, so desist!
יָשִׁית מִמֶּנִּי וְאַבְלִיגָה מְּעָט: — ושית ק׳ ב״א מְעָט	Leave me alone, let me be diverted awhile
21 בְּטֶרֶם אֵלֵךְ וְלֹא אָשׁוּב	21 Before I depart—never to return—
אֶל־אֶרֶץ חֹשֶׁךְ וְצַלְמָוֶת:	For the land of deepest gloom;

[a-a] *Meaning of Heb. uncertain.*

כב אֶרֶץ עֵפָתָה ׀ כְּמוֹ־אֹפֶל
צַלְמָוֶת וְלֹא־סְדָרִים
וַתֹּפַע כְּמוֹ־אֹפֶל׃

22 A land whose light is darkness,
All gloom and disarray,
Whose light is like darkness."

יא

1 וַיַּעַן צֹפַר הַנַּעֲמָתִי וַיֹּאמַר׃

11

Then Zophar the Naamathite said in reply:

2 הֲרֹב דְּבָרִים לֹא יֵעָנֶה
וְאִם־אִישׁ שְׂפָתַיִם יִצְדָּק׃
3 בַּדֶּיךָ מְתִים יַחֲרִישׁוּ
וַתִּלְעַג וְאֵין מַכְלִם׃
4 וַתֹּאמֶר זַךְ לִקְחִי
וּבַר הָיִיתִי בְעֵינֶיךָ׃
5 וְאוּלָם מִי־יִתֵּן אֱלוֹהַּ דַּבֵּר
וְיִפְתַּח שְׂפָתָיו עִמָּךְ׃
6 וְיַגֶּד־לְךָ ׀ תַּעֲלֻמוֹת חָכְמָה
כִּי־כִפְלַיִם לְתוּשִׁיָּה
וְדַע ׀ כִּי־יַשֶּׁה לְךָ אֱלוֹהַּ מֵעֲוֺנֶךָ׃

2 Is a multitude of words unanswerable?
Must a loquacious person be right?
3 Your prattle may silence men;
You may mock without being rebuked,
4 And say, "My doctrine is pure,
And I have been innocent in Your sight."
5 But would that God might speak,
And talk to you Himself.
6 He would tell you the secrets of wisdom,
[a]For there are many sides to sagacity;
And know that God has overlooked for you some of your iniquity.[a]

7 הַחֵקֶר אֱלוֹהַּ תִּמְצָא
אִם עַד־תַּכְלִית שַׁדַּי תִּמְצָא׃
8 גָּבְהֵי שָׁמַיִם מַה־תִּפְעָל
עֲמֻקָּה מִשְּׁאוֹל מַה־תֵּדָע׃
9 אֲרֻכָּה מֵאֶרֶץ מִדָּה
וּרְחָבָה מִנִּי־יָם׃
10 אִם־יַחֲלֹף וְיַסְגִּיר
וְיַקְהִיל וּמִי יְשִׁיבֶנּוּ׃
11 כִּי־הוּא יָדַע מְתֵי־שָׁוְא
וַיַּרְא־אָוֶן וְלֹא יִתְבּוֹנָן׃
12 וְאִישׁ נָבוּב יִלָּבֵב
וְעַיִר פֶּרֶא אָדָם יִוָּלֵד׃

7 Would you discover the mystery of God?
Would you discover the limit of the Almighty?
8 Higher than heaven—what can you do?
Deeper than Sheol—what can you know?
9 Its measure is longer than the earth
And broader than the sea.
10 [a]Should He pass by, or confine,
Or call an assembly, who can stop Him?[a]
11 For He knows deceitful men;
When He sees iniquity does He not discern it?
12 [a]A hollow man will get understanding,
When a wild ass is born to a man.[a]

13 אִם־אַתָּה הֲכִינוֹתָ לִבֶּךָ
וּפָרַשְׂתָּ אֵלָיו כַּפֶּךָ׃
14 אִם־אָוֶן בְּיָדְךָ הַרְחִיקֵהוּ
וְאַל־תַּשְׁכֵּן בְּאֹהָלֶיךָ עַוְלָה׃
15 כִּי־אָז ׀ תִּשָּׂא פָנֶיךָ מִמּוּם
וְהָיִיתָ מֻצָק וְלֹא תִירָא׃
16 כִּי־אַתָּה עָמָל תִּשְׁכָּח

13 But if you direct your mind,
And spread forth your hands toward Him;
14 If there is iniquity with you, remove it;
Do not let injustice reside in your tent.
15 Then, free of blemish, you will hold your head high,
And, [b]when in straits,[b] be unafraid.
16 You will then put your misery out of mind,

a-a *Meaning of Heb. uncertain.*
b-b *Heb.* muṣaq; *other Heb. editions* muṣṣaq, *"you will be firm."*

כְּמַיִם עָבְרוּ תִזְכֹּר׃
17 וּמִצָּהֳרַיִם יָקוּם חָלֶד
תָּעֻפָה כַּבֹּקֶר תִּהְיֶה׃
18 וּבָטַחְתָּ כִּי־יֵשׁ תִּקְוָה
וְחָפַרְתָּ לָבֶטַח תִּשְׁכָּב׃
19 וְרָבַצְתָּ וְאֵין מַחֲרִיד
וְחִלּוּ פָנֶיךָ רַבִּים׃
20 וְעֵינֵי רְשָׁעִים תִּכְלֶינָה
וּמָנוֹס אָבַד מִנְהֶם
וְתִקְוָתָם מַפַּח־נָפֶשׁ׃

Consider it as water that has flowed past.
17 [a]Life will be brighter than noon;[a]
You will shine, you will be like the morning.
18 You will be secure, for there is hope,
[a]And, entrenched,[a] you will rest secure;
19 You will lie down undisturbed;
The great will court your favor.
20 But the eyes of the wicked pine away;
Escape is cut off from them;
They have only their last breath to look forward to.

יב

1 וַיַּעַן אִיּוֹב וַיֹּאמַר׃

12

Then Job said in reply:

2 אָמְנָם כִּי אַתֶּם־עָם
וְעִמָּכֶם תָּמוּת חָכְמָה׃
3 גַּם־לִי לֵבָב ׀ כְּמוֹכֶם
לֹא־נֹפֵל אָנֹכִי מִכֶּם
וְאֶת־מִי־אֵין כְּמוֹ־אֵלֶּה׃
4 שְׂחֹק לְרֵעֵהוּ ׀ אֶהְיֶה
קֹרֵא לֶאֱלוֹהַּ וַיַּעֲנֵהוּ
שְׂחוֹק צַדִּיק תָּמִים׃
5 לַפִּיד בּוּז לְעַשְׁתּוּת שַׁאֲנָן
נָכוֹן לְמוֹעֲדֵי רָגֶל׃

2 Indeed, you are the [voice of] the people,
And wisdom will die with you.
3 But I, like you, have a mind,
And am not less than you.
Who does not know such things?
4 I have become a laughingstock to my friend,
"One who calls to God and is answered,
Blamelessly innocent," a laughingstock.
5 [a]In the thought of the complacent there is contempt for calamity;
It is ready for those whose foot slips.[a]

6 יִשְׁלָיוּ אֹהָלִים ׀ לְשֹׁדְדִים
וּבַטֻּחוֹת לְמַרְגִּיזֵי אֵל
לַאֲשֶׁר הֵבִיא אֱלוֹהַּ בְּיָדוֹ׃

6 Robbers live untroubled in their tents,
And those who provoke God are secure,
[a]Those whom God's hands have produced.[a]

7 וְאוּלָם שְׁאַל־נָא בְהֵמוֹת וְתֹרֶךָּ
וְעוֹף הַשָּׁמַיִם וְיַגֶּד־לָךְ׃
8 אוֹ שִׂיחַ לָאָרֶץ וְתֹרֶךָּ
וִיסַפְּרוּ לְךָ דְּגֵי הַיָּם׃
9 מִי לֹא־יָדַע בְּכָל־אֵלֶּה
כִּי יַד־יְהוָה עָשְׂתָה זֹּאת׃
10 אֲשֶׁר בְּיָדוֹ נֶפֶשׁ כָּל־חָי
וְרוּחַ כָּל־בְּשַׂר־אִישׁ׃
11 הֲלֹא־אֹזֶן מִלִּין תִּבְחָן
וְחֵךְ אֹכֶל יִטְעַם־־לוֹ׃
12 בִּישִׁישִׁים חָכְמָה
וְאֹרֶךְ יָמִים תְּבוּנָה׃

7 But ask the beasts, and they will teach you;
The birds of the sky, they will tell you,
8 Or speak to the earth, it will teach you;
The fish of the sea, they will inform you.
9 Who among all these does not know
That the hand of the LORD has done this?
10 In His hand is every living soul
And the breath of all mankind.
11 Truly, the ear tests arguments
As the palate tastes foods.
12 Is wisdom in the aged
And understanding in the long-lived?

a-a *Meaning of Heb. uncertain.*

13 עִמּוֹ חָכְמָה וּגְבוּרָה
לוֹ עֵצָה וּתְבוּנָה׃
14 הֵן יַהֲרוֹס וְלֹא יִבָּנֶה
יִסְגֹּר עַל־אִישׁ וְלֹא יִפָּתֵחַ׃
15 הֵן יַעְצֹר בַּמַּיִם וְיִבָשׁוּ
וִישַׁלְּחֵם וְיַהַפְכוּ־אָרֶץ׃
16 עִמּוֹ עֹז וְתוּשִׁיָּה
לוֹ שֹׁגֵג וּמַשְׁגֶּה׃
17 מוֹלִיךְ יוֹעֲצִים שׁוֹלָל
וְשֹׁפְטִים יְהוֹלֵל׃
18 מוּסַר מְלָכִים פִּתֵּחַ
וַיֶּאְסֹר אֵזוֹר בְּמָתְנֵיהֶם׃
19 מוֹלִיךְ כֹּהֲנִים שׁוֹלָל
וְאֵתָנִים יְסַלֵּף׃
20 מֵסִיר שָׂפָה לְנֶאֱמָנִים
וְטַעַם זְקֵנִים יִקָּח׃
21 שׁוֹפֵךְ בּוּז עַל־נְדִיבִים
וּמְזִיחַ אֲפִיקִים רִפָּה׃
22 מְגַלֶּה עֲמֻקוֹת מִנִּי־חֹשֶׁךְ בנ״א הק׳ דגושה
וַיֹּצֵא לָאוֹר צַלְמָוֶת׃
23 מַשְׂגִּיא לַגּוֹיִם וַיְאַבְּדֵם
שֹׁטֵחַ לַגּוֹיִם וַיַּנְחֵם׃
24 מֵסִיר לֵב רָאשֵׁי עַם־הָאָרֶץ
וַיַּתְעֵם בְּתֹהוּ לֹא־דָרֶךְ׃
25 יְמַשְׁשׁוּ־חֹשֶׁךְ וְלֹא־אוֹר
וַיַּתְעֵם כַּשִּׁכּוֹר׃

יג
1 הֶן כֹּל רָאֲתָה עֵינִי
שָׁמְעָה אָזְנִי וַתָּבֶן לָהּ׃
2 כְּדַעְתְּכֶם יָדַעְתִּי גַם־אָנִי
לֹא־נֹפֵל אָנֹכִי מִכֶּם׃
3 אוּלָם אֲנִי אֶל־שַׁדַּי אֲדַבֵּר
וְהוֹכֵחַ אֶל־אֵל אֶחְפָּץ׃
4 וְאוּלָם אַתֶּם טֹפְלֵי־שָׁקֶר
רֹפְאֵי אֱלִל כֻּלְּכֶם׃
5 מִי־יִתֵּן הַחֲרֵשׁ תַּחֲרִישׁוּן
וּתְהִי לָכֶם לְחָכְמָה׃
6 שִׁמְעוּ־נָא תוֹכַחְתִּי
וְרִבוֹת שְׂפָתַי הַקְשִׁיבוּ׃

13 With Him are wisdom and courage;
His are counsel and understanding.
14 Whatever He tears down cannot be rebuilt;
Whomever He imprisons cannot be set free.
15 When He holds back the waters, they dry up;
When He lets them loose, they tear up the land.
16 With Him are strength and resourcefulness;
Erring and causing to err are from Him.
17 He makes counselors go about naked[b]
And causes judges to go mad.
18 He undoes the belts of kings,
And fastens loincloths on them.
19 He makes priests go about naked[b],
And leads temple-servants[c] astray.
20 He deprives trusty men of speech,
And takes away the reason of elders.
21 He pours disgrace upon great men,
And loosens the belt of the mighty.
22 He draws mysteries out of the darkness,
And brings obscurities to light.
23 He exalts nations, then destroys them;
He expands nations, then leads them away.
24 He deranges the leaders of the people,
And makes them wander in a trackless waste.
25 They grope without light in the darkness;
He makes them wander as if drunk.

13

My eye has seen all this;
My ear has heard and understood it.
2 What you know, I know also;
I am not less than you.
3 Indeed, I would speak to the Almighty;
I insist on arguing with God.
4 But you invent lies;
All of you are quacks.
5 If you would only keep quiet
It would be considered wisdom on your part.
6 Hear now my arguments,
Listen to my pleading.

[b] *A sign of madness.*
[c] *Cf. Ugaritic* ytnm, *a class of temple servants; others "the mighty."*

7 הַלְאֵל תְּדַבְּרוּ עַוְלָה
וְלוֹ תְּדַבְּרוּ רְמִיָּה׃
8 הֲפָנָיו תִּשָּׂאוּן אִם־לָאֵל תְּרִיבוּן׃

9 הֲטוֹב כִּי־יַחְקֹר אֶתְכֶם
אִם־כְּהָתֵל בֶּאֱנוֹשׁ תְּהָתֵלּוּ בוֹ׃ דגש אחר ת״ג
10 הוֹכֵחַ יוֹכִיחַ אֶתְכֶם
אִם־בַּסֵּתֶר פָּנִים תִּשָּׂאוּן׃
11 הֲלֹא שְׂאֵתוֹ תְּבַעֵת אֶתְכֶם
וּפַחְדּוֹ יִפֹּל עֲלֵיכֶם׃
12 זִכְרֹנֵיכֶם מִשְׁלֵי־אֵפֶר
לְגַבֵּי־חֹמֶר גַּבֵּיכֶם׃

13 הַחֲרִישׁוּ מִמֶּנִּי וַאֲדַבְּרָה־אָנִי
וְיַעֲבֹר עָלַי מָה׃
14 עַל־מָה ׀ אֶשָּׂא בְשָׂרִי בְשִׁנָּי
וְנַפְשִׁי אָשִׂים בְּכַפִּי׃
15 הֵן יִקְטְלֵנִי לֹא אֲיַחֵל לו ק׳
אַךְ־דְּרָכַי אֶל־פָּנָיו אוֹכִיחַ׃
16 גַּם־הוּא־לִי לִישׁוּעָה
כִּי־לֹא לְפָנָיו חָנֵף יָבוֹא׃

17 שִׁמְעוּ שָׁמוֹעַ מִלָּתִי
וְאַחְוָתִי בְּאָזְנֵיכֶם׃
18 הִנֵּה־נָא עָרַכְתִּי מִשְׁפָּט
יָדַעְתִּי כִּי־אֲנִי אֶצְדָּק׃
19 מִי־הוּא יָרִיב עִמָּדִי
כִּי־עַתָּה אַחֲרִישׁ וְאֶגְוָע׃
20 אַךְ־שְׁתַּיִם אַל־תַּעַשׂ עִמָּדִי
אָז מִפָּנֶיךָ לֹא אֶסָּתֵר׃
21 כַּפְּךָ מֵעָלַי הַרְחַק פתח באתנח
וְאֵמָתְךָ אַל־תְּבַעֲתַנִּי׃ פתח בס״פ
22 וּקְרָא וְאָנֹכִי אֶעֱנֶה
אוֹ־אֲדַבֵּר וַהֲשִׁיבֵנִי׃
23 כַּמָּה לִי עֲוֹנוֹת וְחַטָּאוֹת
פִּשְׁעִי וְחַטָּאתִי הֹדִיעֵנִי׃
24 לָמָּה־פָנֶיךָ תַסְתִּיר
וְתַחְשְׁבֵנִי לְאוֹיֵב לָךְ׃
25 הֶעָלֶה נִדָּף תַּעֲרוֹץ

7 Will you speak unjustly on God's behalf?
Will you speak deceitfully for Him?
8 Will you be partial toward Him?
Will you plead God's cause?
9 Will it go well when He examines you?
Will you fool Him as one fools men?
10 He will surely reprove you
If in [a]your heart[a] you are partial toward Him.
11 His threat will terrify you,
And His fear will seize you.
12 Your briefs are empty[b] platitudes;
Your responses are unsubstantial.[c]

13 Keep quiet; I will have my say;
Let what may come upon me.
14 How long! I will take my flesh in my teeth;
I will take my life in my hands.
15 [d]He may well slay me; I may have no hope;[d]
Yet I will argue my case before Him.
16 In this too is my salvation:
That no impious man can come into His presence.

17 Listen closely to my words;
Give ear to my discourse.
18 See now, I have prepared a case;
I know that I will win it.
19 For who is it that would challenge me?
I should then keep silent and expire.
20 But two things do not do to me,
So that I need not hide from You:
21 Remove Your hand from me,
And let not Your terror frighten me.
22 Then summon me and I will respond,
Or I will speak and You reply to me.
23 How many are my iniquities and sins?
Advise me of my transgression and sin.
24 Why do You hide Your face,
And treat me like an enemy?
25 Will You harass a driven leaf,

a-a *Lit. "secret."*
b *Lit. "ashen."*
c *Lit. "clayey."*
d-d *So with* kethib; *others with* qere *"Though He slay me, yet will I trust in Him."*

וְאֶת־קַשׁ יָבֵשׁ תִּרְדֹּף:	Will You pursue dried straw,
26 כִּֽי־תִכְתֹּב עָלַי מְרֹרוֹת	26 That You decree for me bitter things,
וְתוֹרִישֵׁנִי עֲוֺנוֹת נְעוּרָי:	And make me [e]-answer for-[e] the iniquities of my youth,
27 וְתָשֵׂם בַּסַּד ׀ רַגְלַי	27 That You put my feet in the stocks
וְתִשְׁמוֹר כָּל־אָרְחֹתָי	And watch all my ways,
עַל־שָׁרְשֵׁי רַגְלַי תִּתְחַקֶּה:	[f]-Hemming in my footsteps?-[f]
28 וְהוּא כְּרָקָב יִבְלֶה	28 Man wastes away like a rotten thing,
כְּבֶגֶד אֲכָלוֹ עָשׁ:	Like a garment eaten by moths.
יד	14
1 אָדָם יְלוּד אִשָּׁה	Man born of woman is short-lived and sated with trouble.
קְצַר יָמִים וּשְׂבַע־רֹגֶז:	2 He blossoms like a flower and withers;
2 כְּצִיץ יָצָא וַיִּמָּל	He vanishes like a shadow and does not endure.
וַיִּבְרַח כַּצֵּל וְלֹא יַעֲמוֹד:	3 Do You fix Your gaze on such a one?
3 אַף־עַל־זֶה פָּקַחְתָּ עֵינֶךָ	Will You go to law with me?
וְאֹתִי תָבִיא בְמִשְׁפָּט עִמָּךְ:	4 [a]-Who can produce a clean thing out of an unclean one?
4 מִי־יִתֵּן טָהוֹר מִטָּמֵא לֹא אֶחָד:	No one!-[a]
5 אִם־חֲרוּצִים ׀ יָמָיו	5 His days are determined;
מִסְפַּר־חֳדָשָׁיו אִתָּךְ	You know the number of his months;
חֻקָּו עָשִׂיתָ וְלֹא יַעֲבֹר: חקיו ק׳	You have set him limits that he cannot pass.
6 שְׁעֵה מֵעָלָיו וְיֶחְדָּל	6 Turn away from him, that he may be at ease
עַד־יִרְצֶה כְּשָׂכִיר יוֹמוֹ:	Until, like a hireling, he finishes out his day.
7 כִּי יֵשׁ לָעֵץ תִּקְוָה	7 There is hope for a tree;
אִם־יִכָּרֵת וְעוֹד יַחֲלִיף	If it is cut down it will renew itself;
וְיֹנַקְתּוֹ לֹא תֶחְדָּל:	Its shoots will not cease.
8 אִם־יַזְקִין בָּאָרֶץ שָׁרְשׁוֹ	8 If its roots are old in the earth,
וּבֶעָפָר יָמוּת גִּזְעוֹ:	And its stump dies in the ground,
9 מֵרֵיחַ מַיִם יַפְרִחַ	9 At the scent of water it will bud
וְעָשָׂה קָצִיר כְּמוֹ־נָטַע:	And produce branches like a sapling.
10 וְגֶבֶר יָמוּת וַיֶּחֱלָשׁ	10 But mortals languish and die;
וַיִּגְוַע אָדָם וְאַיּוֹ:	Man expires; where is he?
11 אָזְלוּ־מַיִם מִנִּי־יָם	11 The waters of the sea fail,
וְנָהָר יֶחֱרַב וְיָבֵשׁ:	And the river dries up and is parched.
12 וְאִישׁ שָׁכַב וְלֹא־יָקוּם	12 So man lies down never to rise;
עַד־בִּלְתִּי שָׁמַיִם לֹא יָקִיצוּ	He will awake only when the heavens are no more,
וְלֹא יֵעֹרוּ מִשְּׁנָתָם:	Only then be aroused from his sleep.
13 מִי יִתֵּן ׀ בִּשְׁאוֹל תַּצְפִּנֵנִי	13 O that You would hide me in Sheol,
תַּסְתִּירֵנִי עַד־שׁוּב אַפֶּךָ	Conceal me until Your anger passes,

[e-e] *Lit. "inherit."*
[f-f] *Meaning of Heb. uncertain.*

[a-a] *Meaning of Heb. uncertain.*

תָּשִׁית לִי חֹק וְתִזְכְּרֵנִי׃
14 אִם־יָמוּת גֶּבֶר הֲיִחְיֶה
כָּל־יְמֵי צְבָאִי אֲיַחֵל
עַד־בּוֹא חֲלִיפָתִי׃
15 תִּקְרָא וְאָנֹכִי אֶעֱנֶךָּ
לְמַעֲשֵׂה יָדֶיךָ תִכְסֹף׃
16 כִּי־עַתָּה צְעָדַי תִּסְפּוֹר
לֹא תִשְׁמֹר עַל־חַטָּאתִי׃
17 חָתֻם בִּצְרוֹר פִּשְׁעִי
וַתִּטְפֹּל עַל־עֲוֺנִי׃

Set me a fixed time to attend to me.
14 If a man dies, can he live again?
All the time of my service I wait
Until my replacement comes.
15 You would call and I would answer You;
You would set Your heart on Your handiwork.
16 Then You would not count my steps,
Or keep watch over my sin.
17 My transgression would be sealed up in a pouch;
You would coat over my iniquity.

18 וְאוּלָם הַר־נוֹפֵל יִבּוֹל
וְצוּר יֶעְתַּק מִמְּקֹמוֹ׃
19 אֲבָנִים ׀ שָׁחֲקוּ מַיִם
תִּשְׁטֹף־סְפִיחֶיהָ עֲפַר־אָרֶץ
וְתִקְוַת אֱנוֹשׁ הֶאֱבַדְתָּ׃
20 תִּתְקְפֵהוּ לָנֶצַח וַיַּהֲלֹךְ
מְשַׁנֶּה פָנָיו וַתְּשַׁלְּחֵהוּ׃
21 יִכְבְּדוּ בָנָיו וְלֹא יֵדָע
וְיִצְעֲרוּ וְלֹא־יָבִין לָמוֹ׃
22 אַךְ בְּשָׂרוֹ עָלָיו יִכְאָב
וְנַפְשׁוֹ עָלָיו תֶּאֱבָל׃

18 Mountains collapse and crumble;
Rocks are dislodged from their place.
19 Water wears away stone;
Torrents wash away earth;
So you destroy man's hope,
20 You overpower him for ever and he perishes;
You alter his visage and dispatch him.
21 His sons attain honor and he does not know it;
They are humbled and he is not aware of it.
22 He feels only the pain of his flesh,
And his spirit mourns in him.

טו
1 וַיַּעַן אֱלִיפַז הַתֵּימָנִי וַיֹּאמַר׃

15 Eliphaz the Temanite said in reply:

2 הֶחָכָם יַעֲנֶה דַעַת־רוּחַ
וִימַלֵּא קָדִים בִּטְנוֹ׃
3 הוֹכֵחַ בְּדָבָר לֹא יִסְכּוֹן
וּמִלִּים לֹא־יוֹעִיל בָּם׃
4 אַף־אַתָּה תָּפֵר יִרְאָה
וְתִגְרַע שִׂיחָה לִפְנֵי־אֵל׃
5 כִּי־יְאַלֵּף עֲוֺנְךָ פִיךָ
וְתִבְחַר לְשׁוֹן עֲרוּמִים׃
6 יַרְשִׁיעֲךָ פִיךָ וְלֹא־אָנִי
וּשְׂפָתֶיךָ יַעֲנוּ־בָךְ׃

2 Does a wise man answer with windy opinions,
And fill his belly with the east wind?
3 Should he argue with useless talk,
With words that are of no worth?
4 You subvert piety
And restrain prayer to God.
5 Your sinfulness dictates your speech,
So you choose crafty language.
6 Your own mouth condemns you—not I;
Your lips testify against you.

7 הֲרִאישׁוֹן אָדָם תִּוָּלֵד יתיר י׳
וְלִפְנֵי גְבָעוֹת חוֹלָלְתָּ׃
8 הַבְסוֹד אֱלוֹהַּ תִּשְׁמָע בב״א הב׳ בדגש
וְתִגְרַע אֵלֶיךָ חָכְמָה׃
9 מַה־יָּדַעְתָּ וְלֹא נֵדָע

7 Were you the first man born?
Were you created before the hills?
8 Have you listened in on the council of God?
Have you sole possession of wisdom?
9 What do you know that we do not know,

תָּבִין וְלֹא־עִמָּנוּ הוּא׃
10 נַם־שָׂב נַּם־יָשִׁישׁ בָּנוּ
כַּבִּיר מֵאָבִיךָ יָמִים׃
11 הַמְעַט מִמְּךָ תַּנְחֻמוֹת אֵל
וְדָבָר לָאַט עִמָּךְ׃
12 מַה־יִּקָּחֲךָ לִבֶּךָ
וּמַה־יִּרְזְמוּן עֵינֶיךָ׃
13 כִּי־תָשִׁיב אֶל־אֵל רוּחֶךָ
וְהֹצֵאתָ מִפִּיךָ מִלִּין׃
14 מָה־אֱנוֹשׁ כִּי־יִזְכֶּה
וְכִי־יִצְדַּק יְלוּד אִשָּׁה׃
15 הֵן בִּקְדֹשָׁו לֹא יַאֲמִין
וְשָׁמַיִם לֹא־זַכּוּ בְעֵינָיו׃
16 אַף כִּי־נִתְעָב וְנֶאֱלָח
אִישׁ־שֹׁתֶה כַמַּיִם עַוְלָה׃

17 אֲחַוְךָ שְׁמַע־לִי
וְזֶה־חָזִיתִי וַאֲסַפֵּרָה׃
18 אֲשֶׁר־חֲכָמִים יַגִּידוּ
וְלֹא כִחֲדוּ מֵאֲבוֹתָם׃
19 לָהֶם לְבַדָּם נִתְּנָה הָאָרֶץ
וְלֹא־עָבַר זָר בְּתוֹכָם׃
20 כָּל־יְמֵי רָשָׁע הוּא מִתְחוֹלֵל
וּמִסְפַּר שָׁנִים נִצְפְּנוּ לֶעָרִיץ׃
21 קוֹל־פְּחָדִים בְּאָזְנָיו
בַּשָּׁלוֹם שׁוֹדֵד יְבוֹאֶנּוּ׃
22 לֹא־יַאֲמִין שׁוּב מִנִּי־חֹשֶׁךְ
וְצָפוּי הוּא אֱלֵי־חָרֶב׃
23 נֹדֵד הוּא לַלֶּחֶם אַיֵּה
יָדַע ׀ כִּי־נָכוֹן בְּיָדוֹ יוֹם־חֹשֶׁךְ׃

24 יְבַעֲתֻהוּ צַר וּמְצוּקָה
תִּתְקְפֵהוּ כְּמֶלֶךְ ׀ עָתִיד לַכִּידוֹר׃
25 כִּי־נָטָה אֶל־אֵל יָדוֹ
וְאֶל־שַׁדַּי יִתְגַּבָּר׃
26 יָרוּץ אֵלָיו בְּצַוָּאר
בַּעֲבִי גַּבֵּי מָגִנָּיו׃
27 כִּי־כִסָּה פָנָיו בְּחֶלְבּוֹ
וַיַּעַשׂ פִּימָה עֲלֵי־כָסֶל׃

Or understand that we do not?

10 Among us are gray-haired old men,
Older by far than your father.

11 Are God's consolations not enough for you,
And His gentle words to you?

12 How your heart has carried you away,
How your eyes *a*-have failed-*a* you,

13 That you could vent your anger on God,
And let such words out of your mouth!

14 What is man that he can be cleared of guilt,
One born of woman, that he be in the right?

15 He puts no trust in His holy ones;
The heavens are not guiltless in His sight;

16 What then of one loathsome and foul,
Man, who drinks wrongdoing like water!

17 I will hold forth; listen to me;
What I have seen, I will declare—

18 That which wise men have transmitted from their
   fathers,
And have not withheld,

19 To whom alone the land was given,
No stranger passing among them:

20 The wicked man writhes in torment all his days;
Few years are reserved for the ruthless.

21 Frightening sounds fill his ears;
When he is at ease a robber falls upon him.

22 He is never sure he will come back from the dark;
A sword stares him in the face.

23 He wanders about for bread—where is it?
He knows that the day of darkness has been readied for
   him.

24 Troubles terrify him, anxiety overpowers him,
Like a king *a*-expecting a siege.-*a*

25 For he has raised his arm against God
And played the hero against the Almighty.

26 He runs at Him defiantly[b]
a-With his thickly bossed shield.

27 His face is covered with fat
And his loins with blubber.-*a*

---

a-a *Meaning of Heb. uncertain.*
b *Lit. "with neck."*

28 וַיִּשְׁכּוֹן ׀ עָרִים נִכְחָדוֹת
בָּתִּים לֹא־יֵשְׁבוּ לָמוֹ
אֲשֶׁר הִתְעַתְּדוּ לְגַלִּים׃
29 לֹא־יֶעְשַׁר וְלֹא־יָקוּם חֵילוֹ
וְלֹא־יִטֶּה לָאָרֶץ מִנְלָם׃

30 לֹא־יָסוּר ׀ מִנִּי־חֹשֶׁךְ
יֹנַקְתּוֹ תְּיַבֵּשׁ שַׁלְהָבֶת
וְיָסוּר בְּרוּחַ פִּיו׃
31 אַל־יַאֲמֵן בַּשָּׁו נִתְעָה חסר א׳
כִּי־שָׁוְא תִּהְיֶה תְמוּרָתוֹ׃

32 בְּלֹא־יוֹמוֹ תִּמָּלֵא
וְכִפָּתוֹ לֹא רַעֲנָנָה׃
33 יַחְמֹס כַּגֶּפֶן בִּסְרוֹ
וְיַשְׁלֵךְ כַּזַּיִת נִצָּתוֹ׃
34 כִּי־עֲדַת חָנֵף גַּלְמוּד
וְאֵשׁ אָכְלָה אָהֳלֵי־שֹׁחַד׃
35 הָרֹה עָמָל וְיָלֹד אָוֶן
וּבִטְנָם תָּכִין מִרְמָה׃

28 He dwells in cities doomed to ruin,
In houses that shall not be lived in,
That are destined to become heaps of rubble.
29 He will not be rich;
His wealth will not endure;
[a]His produce will not bend to the earth.[a]
30 He will never get away from the darkness;
Flames will sear his shoots;
[a]He will pass away by the breath of His mouth.
31 He will not be trusted;
He will be misled by falsehood,
And falsehood will be his recompense.[a]
32 He will wither before his time,
His boughs never having flourished.
33 He will drop his unripe grapes like a vine;
He will shed his blossoms like an olive tree.
34 For the company of the impious is desolate;
Fire consumes the tents of the briber;
35 For they have conceived mischief, given birth to evil,
And their womb has produced deceit.

טז
1 וַיַּעַן אִיּוֹב וַיֹּאמַר׃

2 שָׁמַעְתִּי כְאֵלֶּה רַבּוֹת
מְנַחֲמֵי עָמָל כֻּלְּכֶם׃
3 הֲקֵץ לְדִבְרֵי־רוּחַ
אוֹ מַה־יַּמְרִיצְךָ כִּי תַעֲנֶה׃
4 גַּם ׀ אָנֹכִי כָּכֶם אֲדַבֵּרָה
לוּ יֵשׁ נַפְשְׁכֶם תַּחַת נַפְשִׁי
אַחְבִּירָה עֲלֵיכֶם בְּמִלִּים
וְאָנִיעָה עֲלֵיכֶם בְּמוֹ רֹאשִׁי׃
5 אֲאַמִּצְכֶם בְּמוֹ־פִי
וְנִיד שְׂפָתַי יַחְשֹׂךְ׃
6 אִם־אֲדַבְּרָה לֹא־יֵחָשֵׂךְ כְּאֵבִי
וְאַחְדְּלָה מַה־מִנִּי יַהֲלֹךְ׃
7 אַךְ־עַתָּה הֶלְאָנִי
הֲשִׁמּוֹתָ כָּל־עֲדָתִי׃
8 וַתִּקְמְטֵנִי לְעֵד הָיָה
וַיָּקָם בִּי כַחֲשִׁי בְּפָנַי יַעֲנֶה׃

16

Job said in reply:

2 I have often heard such things;
You are all mischievous comforters.
3 Have windy words no limit?
What afflicts you that you speak on?
4 I would also talk like you
If you were in my place;
I would barrage you with words,
I would wag my head over you.
5 I would encourage you with words,[a]
My moving lips would bring relief.
6 If I speak, my pain will not be relieved,
And if I do not—what have I lost?
7 Now He has truly worn me out;
You have destroyed my whole community.
8 You have shriveled me;
My gauntness serves as a witness,
And testifies against me.

[a] *Lit. "my mouth."*

9 אַפּ֤וֹ טָרַ֨ף ׀ וַֽיִּשְׂטְמֵ֗נִי
חָרַ֣ק עָלַ֣י בְּשִׁנָּ֑יו
צָרִ֓י ׀ יִלְט֖וֹשׁ עֵינָ֣יו לִֽי׃
10 פָּעֲר֬וּ עָלַ֨י ׀ בְּפִיהֶ֗ם
בְּ֭חֶרְפָּה הִכּ֣וּ לְחָיָ֑י
יַ֝֗חַד עָלַ֥י יִתְמַלָּאֽוּן׃
11 יַסְגִּירֵ֣נִי אֵ֭ל אֶ֣ל עֲוִ֑יל
וְעַל־יְדֵ֖י רְשָׁעִ֣ים יִרְטֵֽנִי׃
12 שָׁלֵ֤ו הָיִ֨יתִי ׀ וַֽיְפַרְפְּרֵ֗נִי
וְאָחַ֣ז בְּ֭עָרְפִּי וַֽיְפַצְפְּצֵ֑נִי
וַיְקִימֵ֥נִי ל֝֗וֹ לְמַטָּרָֽה׃
13 יָסֹ֬בּוּ עָלַ֨י ׀ רַבָּ֗יו
יְפַלַּ֣ח כִּ֭לְיוֹתַי וְלֹ֣א יַחְמֹ֑ל
יִשְׁפֹּ֥ךְ לָ֝אָ֗רֶץ מְרֵרָתִֽי׃
14 יִפְרְצֵ֣נִי פֶ֭רֶץ עַל־פְּנֵי־פָ֑רֶץ ק׳ זעירא
יָרֻ֖ץ עָלַ֣י כְּגִבּֽוֹר׃
15 שַׂ֣ק תָּ֭פַרְתִּי עֲלֵ֣י גִלְדִּ֑י
וְעֹלַ֖לְתִּי בֶעָפָ֣ר קַרְנִֽי׃
16 פָּ֭נַי חֳמַרְמְרָ֣ה מִנִּי־בֶ֑כִי חמרמרו ק׳
וְעַ֖ל עַפְעַפַּ֣י צַלְמָֽוֶת׃
17 עַ֭ל לֹא־חָמָ֣ס בְּכַפָּ֑י
וּתְפִלָּתִ֥י זַכָּֽה׃

18 אֶ֭רֶץ אַל־תְּכַסִּ֣י דָמִ֑י
וְאַל־יְ֝הִ֗י מָ֭קוֹם לְזַעֲקָתִֽי׃
19 גַּם־עַ֭תָּה הִנֵּה־בַשָּׁמַ֣יִם עֵדִ֑י
וְ֝שָׂהֲדִ֗י בַּמְּרוֹמִֽים׃
20 מְלִיצַ֥י רֵעָ֑י
אֶל־אֱ֝ל֗וֹהַּ דָּלְפָ֥ה עֵינִֽי׃
21 וְיוֹכַ֣ח לְגֶ֣בֶר עִם־אֱל֑וֹהַּ
וּבֶן־אָדָ֥ם לְרֵעֵֽהוּ׃
22 כִּֽי־שְׁנ֣וֹת מִסְפָּ֣ר יֶאֱתָ֑יוּ
וְאֹ֖רַח לֹא־אָשׁ֣וּב אֶהֱלֹֽךְ׃

יז

1 רוּחִ֣י חֻ֭בָּלָה יָמַ֣י נִזְעָ֑כוּ
קְבָרִ֥ים לִֽי׃
2 אִם־לֹ֣א הֲ֭תֻלִים עִמָּדִ֑י בנ״א הל׳ דגושה
וּ֝בְהַמְּרוֹתָ֗ם תָּלַ֥ן עֵינִֽי׃ המ׳ דגושה
3 שִֽׂימָה־נָּ֭א עָרְבֵ֣נִי עִמָּ֑ךְ

9 In His anger He tears and persecutes me;
He gnashes His teeth at me;
My foe stabs me with his eyes.
10 They open wide their mouths at me;
Reviling me, they strike my cheeks;
They inflame themselves against me.
11 God hands me over to an evil man,
Thrusts me into the clutches of the wicked.
12 I had been untroubled, and He broke me in pieces;
He took me by the scruff and shattered me;
He set me up as His target;
13 His bowmen surrounded me;
He pierced my kidneys; He showed no mercy;
He spilled my bile onto the ground.
14 He breached me, breach after breach;
He rushed at me like a warrior.
15 I sewed sackcloth over my skin;
I *b-*buried my glory*-b* in the dust.
16 My face is red with weeping;
Darkness covers my eyes
17 *c-*For no injustice on my part
And for the purity of my prayer!*-c*

18 Earth, do not cover my blood;
Let there be no resting place for my outcry!
19 Surely now my witness is in heaven;
He who can testify for me is on high.
20 O my advocates, my fellows,
Before God my eyes shed tears;
21 Let Him arbitrate between a man and God
As between a man and his fellow.
22 For a few more years will pass,
And I shall go the way of no return.

17

1 My spirit is crushed, my days run out;
The graveyard waits for me.

2 Surely mocking men keep me company,
And with their provocations I close my eyes.
3 Come now, stand surety for me!

b-b *Lit. "made my horn enter into."*
c-c *Or "Though I did no injustice,*
And my prayer was pure."

מִי-ה֗וּא לְיָדִ֥י יִתָּקֵֽעַ׃

4 כִּֽי-לִ֭בָּם צָפַ֣נְתָּ מִּשָּׂ֑כֶל
עַל-כֵּ֝֗ן לֹ֣א תְרֹמֵֽם׃

5 לְ֭חֵלֶק יַגִּ֣יד רֵעִ֑ים
וְעֵינֵ֖י בָנָ֣יו תִּכְלֶֽנָה׃

6 וְֽהִצִּגַ֗נִי לִמְשֹׁ֥ל עַמִּ֑ים
וְתֹ֖פֶת לְפָנִ֣ים אֶֽהְיֶֽה׃

7 וַתֵּ֣כַהּ מִכַּ֣עַשׂ עֵינִ֑י
וִֽיצֻרַ֖י כַּצֵּ֣ל כֻּלָּֽם׃

8 יָשֹׁ֣מּוּ יְשָׁרִ֣ים עַל-זֹ֑את
וְ֝נָקִ֗י עַל-חָנֵ֥ף יִתְעֹרָֽר׃

9 וְיֹאחֵ֣ז צַדִּ֣יק דַּרְכּ֑וֹ
וּֽטְהָר-יָ֝דַ֗יִם יֹסִ֥יף אֹֽמֶץ׃ בג"א חט' בשוא

10 וְֽאוּלָ֗ם כֻּלָּ֣ם תָּ֭שֻׁבוּ וּבֹ֣אוּ נָ֑א
וְלֹֽא-אֶמְצָ֖א בָכֶ֣ם חָכָֽם׃

11 יָמַ֣י עָ֭בְרוּ זִמֹּתַ֣י נִתְּק֑וּ
מֽוֹרָשֵׁ֥י לְבָבִֽי׃

12 לַ֭יְלָה לְי֣וֹם יָשִׂ֑ימוּ
א֥וֹר קָ֝ר֗וֹב מִפְּנֵי-חֹֽשֶׁךְ׃

13 אִם-אֲ֭קַוֶּה שְׁא֣וֹל בֵּיתִ֑י
בַּ֝חֹ֗שֶׁךְ רִפַּ֥דְתִּי יְצוּעָֽי׃

14 לַשַּׁ֣חַת קָ֭רָאתִי אָ֣בִי אָ֑תָּה
אִמִּ֥י וַ֝אֲחֹתִ֗י לָֽרִמָּֽה׃

15 וְ֭אַיֵּה אֵפ֣וֹ תִקְוָתִ֑י
וְ֝תִקְוָתִ֗י מִ֣י יְשׁוּרֶֽנָּה׃

16 בַּדֵּ֣י שְׁאֹ֣ל תֵּרַ֑דְנָה סתה באתנח
אִם-יַ֖חַד עַל-עָפָ֣ר נָֽחַת׃

יח

1 וַ֭יַּעַן בִּלְדַּ֥ד הַשֻּׁחִ֗י וַיֹּאמַֽר׃

2 עַד-אָ֤נָה ׀ תְּשִׂימ֣וּן קִנְצֵ֣י לְמִלִּ֑ין
תָּ֝בִ֗ינוּ וְאַחַ֥ר נְדַבֵּֽר׃

3 מַ֭דּוּעַ נֶחְשַׁ֣בְנוּ כַבְּהֵמָ֑ה
נִ֝טְמִ֗ינוּ בְּעֵינֵיכֶֽם׃

4 טֹֽרֵ֥ף נַפְשׁ֗וֹ בְּאַ֫פּ֥וֹ
הַ֭לְמַעַנְךָ תֵּעֲזַב אָ֑רֶץ
וְיֶעְתַּק-צ֝֗וּר מִמְּקֹמֽוֹ׃

Who will give his hand on my behalf?

4 You have hidden understanding from their minds;
Therefore You must not exalt [them].

5 He informs on his friends for a share [of their property],
And his children's eyes pine away.

6 He made me a byword among people;
I have become like Tophet[a] of old.

7 My eyes fail from vexation;
All shapes seem to me like shadows.

8 The upright are amazed at this;
The pure are aroused against the impious.

9 The righteous man holds to his way;
He whose hands are clean grows stronger.

10 But all of you, come back now;
I shall not find a wise man among you.

11 My days are done, my tendons severed,
The strings of my heart.

12 They say that night is day,
That light is here—in the face of darkness.

13 If I must look forward to Sheol as my home,
And make my bed in the dark place,

14 Say to the Pit, "You are my father,"
To the maggots, "Mother," "Sister"—

15 Where, then, is my hope?
Who can see hope for me?

16 Will it descend to Sheol?
Shall we go down together to the dust?

18 Then Bildad the Shuhite said in reply:

2 How long? Put an end to talk!
Consider, and then we shall speak.

3 Why are we thought of as brutes,
Regarded by you as stupid?

4 You who tear yourself to pieces in anger—
Will [a]earth's order be disrupted[a] for your sake?
Will rocks be dislodged from their place?

---

[a] *That consumed children; cf. Jer. 7.31.*

[a-a] *Lit. "the earth be abandoned."*

5 גַּם אוֹר רְשָׁעִים יִדְעָךְ	5 Indeed, the light of the wicked fails;
וְלֹא־יִגַּהּ שְׁבִיב אִשּׁוֹ׃	The flame of his fire does not shine.
6 אוֹר חָשַׁךְ בְּאָהֳלוֹ	6 The light in his tent darkens;
וְנֵרוֹ עָלָיו יִדְעָךְ׃	His lamp fails him.
7 יֵצְרוּ צַעֲדֵי אוֹנוֹ	7 His iniquitous strides are hobbled;
וְתַשְׁלִיכֵהוּ עֲצָתוֹ׃	His schemes overthrow him.
8 כִּי־שֻׁלַּח בְּרֶשֶׁת בְּרַגְלָיו	8 He is led by his feet into the net;
וְעַל־שְׂבָכָה יִתְהַלָּךְ׃	He walks onto the toils.
9 יֹאחֵז בְּעָקֵב פָּח	9 The trap seizes his heel;
יַחֲזֵק עָלָיו צַמִּים׃	The noose tightens on him.
10 טָמוּן בָּאָרֶץ חַבְלוֹ	10 The rope for him lies hidden on the ground;
וּמַלְכֻּדְתּוֹ עֲלֵי נָתִיב׃	His snare, on the path.
11 סָבִיב בִּעֲתֻהוּ בַלָּהוֹת	11 Terrors assault him on all sides
וֶהֱפִיצֻהוּ לְרַגְלָיו׃	And set his feet flying.
12 יְהִי־רָעֵב אֹנוֹ	12 His progeny hunger;
וְאֵיד נָכוֹן לְצַלְעוֹ׃	Disaster awaits his wife.[b]
13 יֹאכַל בַּדֵּי עוֹרוֹ	13 The tendons under his skin are consumed;
יֹאכַל בַּדָּיו בְּכוֹר מָוֶת׃	Death's firstborn consumes his tendons.
14 יִנָּתֵק מֵאָהֳלוֹ מִבְטַחוֹ	14 He is torn from the safety of his tent;
וְתַצְעִדֵהוּ לְמֶלֶךְ בַּלָּהוֹת׃	Terror marches him to the king.[c]
15 תִּשְׁכּוֹן בְּאָהֳלוֹ מִבְּלִי־לוֹ	15 It lodges in his desolate tent;
יְזֹרֶה עַל־נָוֵהוּ גָפְרִית׃	Sulfur is strewn upon his home.
16 מִתַּחַת שָׁרָשָׁיו יִבָשׁוּ	16 His roots below dry up,
וּמִמַּעַל יִמַּל קְצִירוֹ׃	And above, his branches wither.
17 זִכְרוֹ־אָבַד מִנִּי־אָרֶץ	17 All mention of him vanishes from the earth;
וְלֹא־שֵׁם לוֹ עַל־פְּנֵי־חוּץ׃	He has no name abroad.
18 יֶהְדְּפֻהוּ מֵאוֹר אֶל־חֹשֶׁךְ	18 He is thrust from light to darkness,
וּמִתֵּבֵל יְנִדֻּהוּ׃	Driven from the world.
19 לֹא־נִין לוֹ וְלֹא־נֶכֶד בְּעַמּוֹ	19 He has no seed or breed among his people,
וְאֵין שָׂרִיד בִּמְגוּרָיו׃	No survivor where he once lived.
20 עַל־יוֹמוֹ נָשַׁמּוּ אַחֲרֹנִים	20 Generations to come will be appalled at his fate,
וְקַדְמֹנִים אָחֲזוּ שָׂעַר׃	As the previous ones are seized with horror.
21 אַךְ־אֵלֶּה מִשְׁכְּנוֹת עַוָּל	21 "These were the haunts of the wicked;
וְזֶה מְקוֹם לֹא־יָדַע־אֵל׃	Here was the place of him who knew not God."

יט

19

1 וַיַּעַן אִיּוֹב וַיֹּאמַר׃	Job said in reply:
2 עַד־אָנָה תּוֹגְיוּן נַפְשִׁי	2 How long will you grieve my spirit,
וּתְדַכְּאוּנַנִי בְמִלִּים׃	And crush me with words?

[b] *Lit. "rib" (cf. Gen. 2.22); or "stumbling."*
[c] *Viz. of the underworld.*

3 זֶה ׀ עֶשֶׂר פְּעָמִים תַּכְלִימוּנִי
לֹא־תֵבֹשׁוּ תַּהְכְּרוּ־לִי׃
4 וְאַף־אָמְנָם שָׁגִיתִי
אִתִּי תָּלִין מְשׁוּגָתִי׃
5 אִם־אָמְנָם עָלַי תַּגְדִּילוּ
וְתוֹכִיחוּ עָלַי חֶרְפָּתִי׃
6 דְּעוּ־אֵפוֹ כִּי־אֱלוֹהַּ עִוְּתָנִי
וּמְצוּדוֹ עָלַי הִקִּיף׃
7 הֵן אֶצְעַק חָמָס וְלֹא אֵעָנֶה
אֲשַׁוַּע וְאֵין מִשְׁפָּט׃
8 אָרְחִי גָדַר וְלֹא אֶעֱבוֹר
וְעַל־נְתִיבוֹתַי חֹשֶׁךְ יָשִׂים׃
9 כְּבוֹדִי מֵעָלַי הִפְשִׁיט
וַיָּסַר עֲטֶרֶת רֹאשִׁי׃
10 יִתְּצֵנִי סָבִיב וָאֵלַךְ פתח באתנח
וַיַּסַּע כָּעֵץ תִּקְוָתִי׃
11 וַיַּחַר עָלַי אַפּוֹ
וַיַּחְשְׁבֵנִי לוֹ כְצָרָיו׃
12 יַחַד ׀ יָבֹאוּ גְדוּדָיו
וַיָּסֹלּוּ עָלַי דַּרְכָּם
וַיַּחֲנוּ סָבִיב לְאָהֳלִי׃
13 אַחַי מֵעָלַי הִרְחִיק
וְיֹדְעַי אַךְ־זָרוּ מִמֶּנִּי׃
14 חָדְלוּ קְרוֹבָי
וּמְיֻדָּעַי שְׁכֵחוּנִי׃
15 גָּרֵי בֵיתִי וְאַמְהֹתַי לְזָר תַּחְשְׁבֻנִי
נָכְרִי הָיִיתִי בְעֵינֵיהֶם׃

16 לְעַבְדִּי קָרָאתִי וְלֹא יַעֲנֶה
בְּמוֹ־פִי אֶתְחַנֶּן־לוֹ׃
17 רוּחִי זָרָה לְאִשְׁתִּי
וְחַנּוֹתִי לִבְנֵי בִטְנִי׃
18 גַּם־עֲוִילִים מָאֲסוּ בִי
אָקוּמָה וַיְדַבְּרוּ־בִי׃
19 תִּעֲבוּנִי כָּל־מְתֵי סוֹדִי
וְזֶה־אָהַבְתִּי נֶהְפְּכוּ־בִי׃
20 בְּעוֹרִי וּבִבְשָׂרִי דָּבְקָה עַצְמִי
וָאֶתְמַלְּטָה בְּעוֹר שִׁנָּי׃

21 חָנֻּנִי חָנֻּנִי אַתֶּם רֵעָי
כִּי יַד־אֱלוֹהַּ נָגְעָה בִּי׃

3 [a]Time and again[a] you humiliate me,
And are not ashamed to abuse me.
4 If indeed I have erred,
My error remains with me.
5 Though you are overbearing toward me,
Reproaching me with my disgrace,
6 Yet know that God has wronged me;
He has thrown up siege works around me.
7 I cry, "Violence!" but am not answered;
I shout, but can get no justice.
8 He has barred my way; I cannot pass;
He has laid darkness upon my path.
9 He has stripped me of my glory,
Removed the crown from my head.
10 He tears down every part of me; I perish;
He uproots my hope like a tree.
11 He kindles His anger against me;
He regards me as one of His foes.
12 His troops advance together;
They build their road toward me
And encamp around my tent.
13 He alienated my kin from me;
My acquaintances disown me.
14 My relatives are gone;
My friends have forgotten me.
15 My dependents and maidservants regard me as a stranger;
I am an outsider to them.

16 I summon my servant but he does not respond;
I must myself entreat him.
17 My odor is repulsive to my wife;
I am loathsome to my children.
18 Even youngsters disdain me;
When I rise, they speak against me.
19 All my bosom friends detest me;
Those I love have turned against me.
20 My bones stick to my skin and flesh;
I escape with the skin of my teeth.

21 Pity me, pity me! You are my friends;
For the hand of God has struck me!

a-a *Lit.* *"Ten times."*

22 לָמָּה תִּרְדְּפֻנִי כְמוֹ־אֵל
וּמִבְּשָׂרִי לֹא תִשְׂבָּעוּ׃
23 מִי־יִתֵּן אֵפוֹ וְיִכָּתְבוּן מִלָּי
מִי־יִתֵּן בַּסֵּפֶר וְיֻחָקוּ׃
24 בְּעֵט־בַּרְזֶל וְעֹפָרֶת
לָעַד בַּצּוּר יֵחָצְבוּן׃
25 וַאֲנִי יָדַעְתִּי גֹּאֲלִי חָי
וְאַחֲרוֹן עַל־עָפָר יָקוּם׃
26 וְאַחַר עוֹרִי נִקְּפוּ־זֹאת
וּמִבְּשָׂרִי אֶחֱזֶה אֱלוֹהַּ׃
27 אֲשֶׁר אֲנִי ׀ אֶחֱזֶה־לִּי
וְעֵינַי רָאוּ וְלֹא־זָר
כָּלוּ כִלְיֹתַי בְּחֵקִי׃
28 כִּי תֹאמְרוּ מַה־נִּרְדָּף־לוֹ
וְשֹׁרֶשׁ דָּבָר נִמְצָא־בִי׃
29 גּוּרוּ לָכֶם ׀ מִפְּנֵי־חֶרֶב
כִּי־חֵמָה עֲוֺנוֹת חָרֶב
לְמַעַן תֵּדְעוּן שַׁדִּין׃ שדון ק׳

22 Why do you pursue me like God,
b-Maligning me insatiably?-*b*
23 O that my words were written down;
Would they were inscribed in a record,
24 Incised on a rock forever
With iron stylus and lead!
25 But I know that my Vindicator lives;
In the end He will testify on earth—
26 This, after my skin will have been peeled off.
But I would behold God while still in my flesh,
27 I myself, not another, would behold Him;
Would see with my own eyes:
My heart[c] pines within me.
28 You say, "How do we persecute him?
The root of the matter is in him."[d]
29 Be in fear of the sword,
For [your] fury is iniquity worthy of the sword;
Know there is a judgment!

כ
1 וַיַּעַן צֹפַר הַנַּעֲמָתִי וַיֹּאמַר׃

20

Zophar the Naamathite said in reply:

2 לָכֵן שְׂעִפַּי יְשִׁיבוּנִי
וּבַעֲבוּר חוּשִׁי בִי׃
3 מוּסַר כְּלִמָּתִי אֶשְׁמָע
וְרוּחַ מִבִּינָתִי יַעֲנֵנִי׃
4 הֲזֹאת יָדַעְתָּ מִנִּי־עַד
מִנִּי שִׂים אָדָם עֲלֵי־אָרֶץ׃
5 כִּי רִנְנַת רְשָׁעִים מִקָּרוֹב
וְשִׂמְחַת חָנֵף עֲדֵי־רָגַע׃
6 אִם־יַעֲלֶה לַשָּׁמַיִם שִׂיאוֹ
וְרֹאשׁוֹ לָעָב יַגִּיעַ׃
7 כְּגֶלְלוֹ לָנֶצַח יֹאבֵד
רֹאָיו יֹאמְרוּ אַיּוֹ׃
8 כַּחֲלוֹם יָעוּף וְלֹא יִמְצָאֻהוּ
וְיֻדַּד כְּחֶזְיוֹן לָיְלָה׃
9 עַיִן שְׁזָפַתּוּ וְלֹא תוֹסִיף
וְלֹא־עוֹד תְּשׁוּרֶנּוּ מְקוֹמוֹ׃
10 בָּנָיו יְרַצּוּ דַלִּים

2 In truth, my thoughts urge me to answer
(It is because of my feelings
3 When I hear reproof that insults me);
A spirit out of my understanding makes me reply:
4 Do you not know this, that from time immemorial,
Since man was set on earth,
5 The joy of the wicked has been brief,
The happiness of the impious, fleeting?
6 Though he grows as high as the sky,
His head reaching the clouds,
7 He perishes forever, like his dung;
Those who saw him will say, "Where is he?"
8 He flies away like a dream and cannot be found;
He is banished like a night vision.
9 Eyes that glimpsed him do so no more;
They cannot see him in his place any longer.
10 His sons ingratiate themselves with the poor;

b-b *Lit. "You are not satisfied with my flesh."*
c *Lit. "kidneys."*
d *With many mss. and versions; printed editions, "me."*

וְיָדָיו תָּשֵׁבְנָה אוֹנוֹ׃	His own hands must give back his wealth.
11 עַצְמוֹתָיו מָלְאוּ עֲלוּמָו עלומיו ק׳	11 His bones, still full of vigor,
וְעִמּוֹ עַל־עָפָר תִּשְׁכָּב׃	Lie down in the dust with him.
12 אִם־תַּמְתִּיק בְּפִיו רָעָה	12 Though evil is sweet to his taste,
יַכְחִידֶנָּה תַּחַת לְשׁוֹנוֹ׃	And he conceals it under his tongue;
13 יַחְמֹל עָלֶיהָ וְלֹא יַעַזְבֶנָּה	13 Though he saves it, does not let it go,
וְיִמְנָעֶנָּה בְּתוֹךְ חִכּוֹ׃	Holds it inside his mouth,
14 לַחְמוֹ בְּמֵעָיו נֶהְפָּךְ	14 His food in his bowels turns
מְרוֹרַת פְּתָנִים בְּקִרְבּוֹ׃	Into asps' venom within him.
15 חַיִל בָּלַע וַיְקִאֶנּוּ	15 The riches he swallows he vomits;
מִבִּטְנוֹ יֹרִשֶׁנּוּ אֵל׃	God empties it out of his stomach.
16 רֹאשׁ־פְּתָנִים יִינָק	16 He sucks the poison of asps;
תַּהַרְגֵהוּ לְשׁוֹן אֶפְעֶה׃	The tongue of the viper kills him.
17 אַל־יֵרֶא בִפְלַגּוֹת	17 Let him not enjoy the streams,
נַהֲרֵי נַחֲלֵי דְבַשׁ וְחֶמְאָה׃	The rivers of honey, the brooks of cream.
18 מֵשִׁיב יָגָע וְלֹא יִבְלָע	18 He will give back the goods unswallowed;
כְּחֵיל תְּמוּרָתוֹ וְלֹא יַעֲלֹס׃	The value of the riches, undigested.
19 כִּי־רִצַּץ עָזַב דַּלִּים	19 Because he crushed and tortured the poor,
בַּיִת גָּזַל וְלֹא יִבֶנֵהוּ׃	He will not build up the house he took by force.
20 כִּי ׀ לֹא־יָדַע שָׁלֵו בְּבִטְנוֹ	20 He will know no peace with his children;
בַּחֲמוּדוֹ לֹא יְמַלֵּט׃	He will not preserve one of his dear ones.
21 אֵין־שָׂרִיד לְאָכְלוֹ	21 With no survivor to enjoy it,
עַל־כֵּן לֹא־יָחִיל טוּבוֹ׃	His fortune will not prosper.
22 בִּמְלֹאות שִׂפְקוֹ יֵצֶר לוֹ יתיר ו׳	22 When he has all he wants, trouble will come;
כָּל־־יַד עָמֵל תְּבֹאֶנּוּ׃	Misfortunes of all kinds will batter him.
23 יְהִי ׀ לְמַלֵּא בִטְנוֹ	23 Let that fill his belly;
יְשַׁלַּח־־בּוֹ חֲרוֹן אַפּוֹ	Let Him loose His burning anger at him,
וְיַמְטֵר עָלֵימוֹ בִּלְחוּמוֹ׃	And rain down His weapons upon him.
24 יִבְרַח מִנֵּשֶׁק בַּרְזֶל	24 Fleeing from iron arrows,
תַּחְלְפֵהוּ קֶשֶׁת נְחוּשָׁה׃	He is shot through from a bow of bronze.
25 שָׁלַף וַיֵּצֵא מִגֵּוָה	25 Brandished and run through his body,
וּבָרָק מִמְּרֹרָתוֹ	The blade, through his gall,
יַהֲלֹךְ עָלָיו אֵמִים׃	Strikes terror into him.
26 כָּל־חֹשֶׁךְ טָמוּן לִצְפּוּנָיו	26 Utter darkness waits for his treasured ones;
תְּאָכְלֵהוּ אֵשׁ לֹא־־נֻפָּח	A fire fanned by no man will consume him;
יֵרַע שָׂרִיד בְּאָהֳלוֹ׃ מלעיל	Who survives in his tent will be crushed.
27 יְגַלּוּ שָׁמַיִם עֲוֹנוֹ	27 Heaven will expose his iniquity;
וְאֶרֶץ מִתְקוֹמָמָה לוֹ׃	Earth will rise up against him.
28 יִגֶל יְבוּל בֵּיתוֹ	28 His household will be cast forth by a flood,
נִגָּרוֹת בְּיוֹם אַפּוֹ׃	Spilled out on the day of His wrath.
29 זֶה ׀ חֵלֶק־אָדָם רָשָׁע ׀ מֵאֱלֹהִים	29 This is the wicked man's portion from God,
וְנַחֲלַת אִמְרוֹ מֵאֵל׃	The lot God has ordained for him.

כא

1 וַיַּעַן אִיּוֹב וַיֹּאמַר׃

2 שִׁמְעוּ שָׁמוֹעַ מִלָּתִי
וּתְהִי־זֹאת תַּנְחוּמֹתֵיכֶם׃
3 שָׂאוּנִי וְאָנֹכִי אֲדַבֵּר
וְאַחַר דַּבְּרִי תַלְעִיג׃
4 הֶאָנֹכִי לְאָדָם שִׂיחִי
וְאִם־מַדּוּעַ לֹא־תִקְצַר רוּחִי׃
5 פְּנוּ־אֵלַי וְהָשַׁמּוּ פתח באתנח בנ״א הה׳ בק״ח
וְשִׂימוּ יָד עַל־פֶּה׃ והש׳ דגושה או הה׳ בח״ק
6 וְאִם־זָכַרְתִּי וְנִבְהָלְתִּי
וְאָחַז בְּשָׂרִי פַּלָּצוּת׃

7 מַדּוּעַ רְשָׁעִים יִחְיוּ
עָתְקוּ גַּם־גָּבְרוּ חָיִל׃
8 זַרְעָם ׀ נָכוֹן לִפְנֵיהֶם עִמָּם
וְצֶאֱצָאֵיהֶם לְעֵינֵיהֶם׃
9 בָּתֵּיהֶם שָׁלוֹם מִפָּחַד
וְלֹא־שֵׁבֶט אֱלוֹהַּ עֲלֵיהֶם׃
10 שׁוֹרוֹ עִבַּר וְלֹא יַגְעִל
תְּפַלֵּט פָּרָתוֹ וְלֹא תְשַׁכֵּל׃
11 יְשַׁלְּחוּ כַצֹּאן עֲוִילֵיהֶם
וְיַלְדֵיהֶם יְרַקֵּדוּן׃
12 יִשְׂאוּ כְּתֹף וְכִנּוֹר
וְיִשְׂמְחוּ לְקוֹל עוּגָב׃
13 יְבַלּוּ בַטּוֹב יְמֵיהֶם יכלו ק׳
וּבְרֶגַע שְׁאוֹל יֵחָתּוּ׃
14 וַיֹּאמְרוּ לָאֵל סוּר מִמֶּנּוּ
וְדַעַת דְּרָכֶיךָ לֹא חָפָצְנוּ׃
15 מַה־שַּׁדַּי כִּי־נַעַבְדֶנּוּ
וּמַה־נּוֹעִיל כִּי נִפְגַּע־בּוֹ׃
16 הֵן לֹא בְיָדָם טוּבָם
עֲצַת רְשָׁעִים רָחֲקָה מֶנִּי׃
17 כַּמָּה ׀ נֵר־רְשָׁעִים יִדְעָךְ קמץ בלא אס״ף
וְיָבֹא עָלֵימוֹ אֵידָם
חֲבָלִים יְחַלֵּק בְּאַפּוֹ׃
18 יִהְיוּ כְּתֶבֶן לִפְנֵי־רוּחַ
וּכְמֹץ גְּנָבַתּוּ סוּפָה׃
19 אֱלוֹהַּ יִצְפֹּן־לְבָנָיו אוֹנוֹ
יְשַׁלֵּם אֵלָיו וְיֵדָע׃

21 Job said in reply:

2 Listen well to what I say,
And let that be your consolation.
3 Bear with me while I speak,
And after I have spoken, you may mock.
4 Is my complaint directed toward a man?
Why should I not lose my patience?
5 Look at me and be appalled,
And clap your hand to your mouth.
6 When I think of it I am terrified;
My body is seized with shuddering.

7 Why do the wicked live on,
Prosper and grow wealthy?
8 Their children are with them always,
And they see their children's children.
9 Their homes are secure, without fear;
They do not feel the rod of God.
10 Their bull breeds and does not fail;
Their cow calves and never miscarries;
11 They let their infants run loose like sheep,
And their children skip about.
12 They sing to the music of timbrel and lute,
And revel to the tune of the pipe;
13 They spend their days in happiness,
And go down to Sheol in peace.
14 They say to God, "Leave us alone,
We do not want to learn Your ways;
15 What is Shaddai that we should serve Him?
What will we gain by praying to Him?"
16 Their happiness is not their own doing.
(The thoughts of the wicked are beyond me!)
17 How seldom does the lamp of the wicked fail,
Does the calamity they deserve befall them,
Does He apportion [their] lot in anger!
18 Let them become like straw in the wind,
Like chaff carried off by a storm.
19 [You say,]"God is reserving his punishment for his sons";
Let it be paid back to him that he may feel it,

²⁰ יִרְא֣וּ עֵינָ֣יו כִּידֹ֑ו *עיניו ק׳*
וּֽמֵחֲמַ֖ת שַׁדַּ֣י יִשְׁתֶּֽה׃

²¹ כִּ֤י מַה־חֶפְצֹ֣ו בְּבֵיתֹ֣ו אַחֲרָ֑יו
וּמִסְפַּ֖ר חֳדָשָׁ֣יו חֻצָּֽצוּ׃

²² הַלְאֵ֥ל יְלַמֶּד־דָּ֑עַת
וְ֝ה֗וּא רָמִ֥ים יִשְׁפֹּֽוט׃

²³ זֶ֗ה יָ֭מוּת בְּעֶ֣צֶם תֻּמֹּ֑ו
כֻּ֝לֹּ֗ו שַׁלְאֲנַ֥ן וְשָׁלֵֽיו׃

²⁴ עֲ֭טִינָיו מָלְא֣וּ חָלָ֑ב
וּמֹ֖חַ עַצְמֹותָ֣יו יְשֻׁקֶּֽה׃

²⁵ וְזֶ֗ה יָ֭מוּת בְּנֶ֣פֶשׁ מָרָ֑ה
וְלֹֽא־אָ֝כַ֗ל בַּטֹּובָֽה׃

²⁶ יַ֭חַד עַל־עָפָ֣ר יִשְׁכָּ֑בוּ
וְ֝רִמָּ֗ה תְּכַסֶּ֥ה עֲלֵיהֶֽם׃

²⁷ הֵ֣ן יָ֭דַעְתִּי מַחְשְׁבֹֽותֵיכֶ֑ם
וּ֝מְזִמֹּ֗ות עָלַ֥י תַּחְמֹֽסוּ׃

²⁸ כִּ֤י תֹֽאמְר֗וּ אַיֵּ֥ה בֵית־נָדִ֑יב
וְ֝אַיֵּ֗ה אֹ֤הֶל ׀ מִשְׁכְּנֹ֬ות רְשָׁעִֽים׃

²⁹ הֲלֹ֣א שְׁ֭אֶלְתֶּם עֹ֣ובְרֵי דָ֑רֶךְ
וְ֝אֹתֹתָ֗ם לֹ֣א תְנַכֵּֽרוּ׃

³⁰ כִּ֤י לְיֹ֣ום אֵ֭יד יֵחָ֣שֶׂךְ רָ֑ע
לְיֹ֖ום עֲבָרֹ֣ות יוּבָֽלוּ׃

³¹ מִֽי־יַגִּ֣יד עַל־פָּנָ֣יו דַּרְכֹּ֑ו
וְהֽוּא־עָ֝שָׂ֗ה מִ֣י יְשַׁלֶּם־לֹֽו׃

³² וְ֭הוּא לִקְבָרֹ֣ות יוּבָ֑ל
וְֽעַל־גָּדִ֥ישׁ יִשְׁקֹֽוד׃

³³ מָֽתְקוּ־לֹ֗ו רִגְבֵ֫י נָ֥חַל
וְ֭אַחֲרָיו כָּל־אָדָ֣ם יִמְשֹׁ֑וךְ
וּ֝לְפָנָ֗יו אֵ֣ין מִסְפָּֽר׃

³⁴ וְ֭אֵיךְ תְּנַחֲמ֣וּנִי הָ֑בֶל
וּ֝תְשֽׁוּבֹתֵיכֶ֗ם נִשְׁאַר־מָֽעַל׃

כב

¹ וַ֭יַּעַן אֱלִיפַ֥ז הַֽתֵּמָנִ֗י וַיֹּאמַֽר׃

² הַלְאֵ֥ל יִסְכָּן־גָּ֑בֶר
כִּֽי־יִסְכֹּ֖ן עָלֵ֣ימֹו מַשְׂכִּֽיל׃

³ הַחֵ֣פֶץ לְ֭שַׁדַּי כִּ֣י תִצְדָּ֑ק
וְאִם־בֶּ֝֗צַע כִּֽי־תַתֵּ֥ם דְּרָכֶֽיךָ׃

⁴ הֲֽ֭מִיִּרְאָ֣תְךָ יֹכִיחֶ֑ךָ
יָבֹ֥וא עִ֝מְּךָ֗ בַּמִּשְׁפָּֽט׃

---

²⁰ Let his eyes see his own ruin,
And let him drink the wrath of Shaddai!

²¹ For what does he care about the fate of his family,
When his number of months runs out?

²² Can God be instructed in knowledge,
He who judges on high?

²³ One man dies in robust health,
All tranquil and untroubled;

²⁴ His pails are full of milk;
The marrow of his bones is juicy.

²⁵ Another dies embittered,
Never having tasted happiness.

²⁶ They both lie in the dust
And are covered with worms.

²⁷ Oh, I know your thoughts,
And the tactics you will devise against me.

²⁸ You will say, "Where is the house of the great man—
And where the tent in which the wicked dwelled?"

²⁹ You must have consulted the wayfarers;
You cannot deny their evidence.

³⁰ For the evil man is spared on the day of calamity,
On the day when wrath is led forth.

³¹ Who will upbraid him to his face?
Who will requite him for what he has done?

³² He is brought to the grave,
While a watch is kept at his tomb.

³³ The clods of the wadi are sweet to him,
Everyone follows behind him,
Innumerable are those who precede him.

³⁴ Why then do you offer me empty consolation?
Of your replies only the perfidy remains.

22 Eliphaz the Temanite said in reply:

² Can a man be of use to God,
A wise man benefit Him?

³ Does Shaddai gain if you are righteous?
Does He profit if your conduct is blameless?

⁴ Is it because of your piety that He arraigns you,
And enters into judgment with you?

5 הֲלֹא רָעָתְךָ רַבָּה
וְאֵין־קֵץ לַעֲוֺנֹתֶיךָ׃
6 כִּי־תַחְבֹּל אַחֶיךָ חִנָּם
וּבִגְדֵי עֲרוּמִּים תַּפְשִׁיט׃ דגש אחר שורק
7 לֹא־מַיִם עָיֵף תַּשְׁקֶה
וּמֵרָעֵב תִּמְנַע־לָחֶם׃
8 וְאִישׁ זְרוֹעַ לוֹ הָאָרֶץ
וּנְשׂוּא פָנִים יֵשֶׁב בָּהּ׃
9 אַלְמָנוֹת שִׁלַּחְתָּ רֵיקָם
וּזְרֹעוֹת יְתֹמִים יְדֻכָּא׃
10 עַל־כֵּן סְבִיבוֹתֶיךָ פַחִים
וִיבַהֶלְךָ פַּחַד פִּתְאוֹם׃
11 אוֹ־חֹשֶׁךְ לֹא־תִרְאֶה
וְשִׁפְעַת־מַיִם תְּכַסֶּךָּ׃

12 הֲלֹא־אֱלוֹהַּ גֹּבַהּ שָׁמָיִם
וּרְאֵה רֹאשׁ כּוֹכָבִים כִּי־רָמּוּ׃ בנ״א המ׳ דגושה
13 וְאָמַרְתָּ מַה־יָּדַע אֵל
הַבְעַד עֲרָפֶל יִשְׁפּוֹט׃
14 עָבִים סֵתֶר־לוֹ וְלֹא יִרְאֶה
וְחוּג שָׁמַיִם יִתְהַלָּךְ׃
15 הַאֹרַח עוֹלָם תִּשְׁמוֹר
אֲשֶׁר דָּרְכוּ מְתֵי־אָוֶן׃ חצי הספר בפסוקים
16 אֲשֶׁר־קֻמְּטוּ וְלֹא־עֵת
נָהָר יוּצַק יְסוֹדָם׃
17 הָאֹמְרִים לָאֵל סוּר מִמֶּנּוּ
וּמַה־יִּפְעַל שַׁדַּי לָמוֹ׃
18 וְהוּא מִלֵּא בָתֵּיהֶם טוֹב
וַעֲצַת רְשָׁעִים רָחֲקָה מֶנִּי׃
19 יִרְאוּ צַדִּיקִים וְיִשְׂמָחוּ
וְנָקִי יִלְעַג־לָמוֹ׃
20 אִם־לֹא נִכְחַד קִימָנוּ
וְיִתְרָם אָכְלָה אֵשׁ׃

21 הַסְכֶּן־נָא עִמּוֹ וּשְׁלָם
בָּהֶם תְּבוֹאַתְךָ טוֹבָה׃
22 קַח־נָא מִפִּיו תּוֹרָה
וְשִׂים אֲמָרָיו בִּלְבָבֶךָ׃
23 אִם־תָּשׁוּב עַד־שַׁדַּי תִּבָּנֶה
תַּרְחִיק עַוְלָה מֵאָהֳלֶיךָ׃
24 וְשִׁית־עַל־עָפָר בָּצֶר

5 You know that your wickedness is great,
And that your iniquities have no limit.
6 You exact pledges from your fellows without reason,
And leave them naked, stripped of their clothes;
7 You do not give the thirsty water to drink;
You deny bread to the hungry.
8 The land belongs to the strong;
The privileged occupy it.
9 You have sent away widows empty-handed;
The strength of the fatherless is broken.
10 Therefore snares are all around you,
And sudden terrors frighten you,
11 Or darkness, so you cannot see;
A flood of waters covers you.

12 God is in the heavenly heights;
See the highest stars, how lofty!
13 You say, "What can God know?
Can He govern through the dense cloud?
14 The clouds screen Him so He cannot see
As He moves about the circuit of heaven."
15 Have you observed the immemorial path
That evil men have trodden;
16 How they were shriveled up before their time
And their foundation poured out like a river?
17 They said to God, "Leave us alone;
What can Shaddai do about it?"
18 But it was He who filled their houses with good things.
(The thoughts of the wicked are beyond me!)
19 The righteous, seeing it,[a] rejoiced;
The innocent laughed with scorn.
20 Surely their substance was destroyed,
And their remnant consumed by fire.

21 Be close to Him and wholehearted;
Good things will come to you thereby.
22 Accept instruction from His mouth;
Lay up His words in your heart.
23 If you return to Shaddai you will be restored,
If you banish iniquity from your tent;
24 If you regard treasure as dirt,

[a] *Referring to v. 16.*

וּבְצוּר נְחָלִים אוֹפִיר׃	Ophir-gold as stones of the wadi,
25 וְהָיָה שַׁדַּי בְּצָרֶיךָ	25 And Shaddai be your treasure
וְכֶסֶף תּוֹעָפוֹת לָךְ׃	And precious silver for you,
26 כִּי־אָז עַל־שַׁדַּי תִּתְעַנָּג	26 When you seek the favor of Shaddai,
וְתִשָּׂא אֶל־אֱלוֹהַּ פָּנֶיךָ׃	And lift up your face to God,
27 תַּעְתִּיר אֵלָיו וְיִשְׁמָעֶךָּ	27 You will pray to Him, and He will listen to you,
וּנְדָרֶיךָ תְשַׁלֵּם׃	And you will pay your vows.
28 וְתִגְזַר־אֹמֶר וְיָקָם לָךְ	28 You will decree and it will be fulfilled,
וְעַל־דְּרָכֶיךָ נָגַהּ אוֹר׃	And light will shine upon your affairs.
29 כִּי־הִשְׁפִּילוּ וַתֹּאמֶר גֵּוָה	29 When others sink low, you will say it is pride;
וְשַׁח עֵינַיִם יוֹשִׁעַ׃	For He saves the humble.
30 יְמַלֵּט אִי־נָקִי	30 He will deliver the guilty;
וְנִמְלַט בְּבֹר כַּפֶּיךָ׃	He will be delivered through the cleanness of your hands.

כג — 23

1 וַיַּעַן אִיּוֹב וַיֹּאמַר׃	Job said in reply:

2 גַּם־הַיּוֹם מְרִי שִׂחִי	2 Today again my complaint is bitter;
יָדִי כָּבְדָה עַל־אַנְחָתִי׃	[a]My strength is spent[a] on account of my groaning.
3 מִי־יִתֵּן יָדַעְתִּי וְאֶמְצָאֵהוּ	3 Would that I knew how to reach Him,
אָבוֹא עַד־תְּכוּנָתוֹ׃	How to get to His dwelling-place.
4 אֶעֶרְכָה לְפָנָיו מִשְׁפָּט	4 I would set out my case before Him
וּפִי אֲמַלֵּא תוֹכָחוֹת׃	And fill my mouth with arguments.
5 אֵדְעָה מִלִּים יַעֲנֵנִי	5 I would learn what answers He had for me
וְאָבִינָה מַה־יֹּאמַר לִי׃	And know how He would reply to me.
6 הַבְּרָב־כֹּחַ יָרִיב עִמָּדִי	6 Would He contend with me overbearingly?
לֹא אַךְ־הוּא יָשִׂם בִּי׃	Surely He would not accuse me!
7 שָׁם יָשָׁר נוֹכָח עִמּוֹ	7 There the upright would be cleared by Him,
וַאֲפַלְּטָה לָנֶצַח מִשֹּׁפְטִי׃	And I would escape forever from my judge.

8 הֵן קֶדֶם אֶהֱלֹךְ וְאֵינֶנּוּ	8 But if I go East—He is not there;
וְאָחוֹר וְלֹא־אָבִין לוֹ׃	West—I still do not perceive Him;
9 שְׂמֹאול בַּעֲשֹׂתוֹ וְלֹא־אָחַז מלעיל	9 North—since He is concealed, I do not behold Him;
יַעְטֹף יָמִין וְלֹא אֶרְאֶה׃	South—He is hidden, and I cannot see Him.
10 כִּי־יָדַע דֶּרֶךְ עִמָּדִי	10 But He knows the way I take;
בְּחָנַנִי כַּזָּהָב אֵצֵא׃	Would He assay me, I should emerge pure as gold.
11 בַּאֲשֻׁרוֹ אָחֲזָה רַגְלִי	11 I have followed in His tracks,
דַּרְכּוֹ שָׁמַרְתִּי וְלֹא־אָט׃	Kept His way without swerving,
12 מִצְוַת שְׂפָתָיו וְלֹא אָמִישׁ	12 I have not deviated from what His lips commanded;
מֵחֻקִּי צָפַנְתִּי אִמְרֵי־פִיו׃	I have treasured His words more than my daily bread.
13 וְהוּא בְאֶחָד וּמִי יְשִׁיבֶנּוּ	13 He is one; who can dissuade Him?

[a-a] *Lit. "My hand is heavy."*

וְנַפְשׁוֹ אִוְּתָה וַיָּעַשׂ׃
14 כִּי יַשְׁלִים חֻקִּי
וְכָהֵנָּה רַבּוֹת עִמּוֹ׃
15 עַל־כֵּן מִפָּנָיו אֶבָּהֵל
אֶתְבּוֹנֵן וְאֶפְחַד מִמֶּנּוּ׃
16 וְאֵל הֵרַךְ לִבִּי
וְשַׁדַּי הִבְהִילָנִי׃
17 כִּי־לֹא נִצְמַתִּי מִפְּנֵי־חֹשֶׁךְ
וּמִפָּנַי כִּסָּה־אֹפֶל׃

כד
1 מַדּוּעַ מִשַּׁדַּי לֹא־נִצְפְּנוּ עִתִּים
וְיֹדְעָו לֹא־חָזוּ יָמָיו׃ וידעיו ק׳
2 גְּבֻלוֹת יַשִּׂיגוּ
עֵדֶר גָּזְלוּ וַיִּרְעוּ׃
3 חֲמוֹר יְתוֹמִים יִנְהָגוּ
יַחְבְּלוּ שׁוֹר אַלְמָנָה׃
4 יַטּוּ אֶבְיֹנִים מִדָּרֶךְ
יַחַד חֻבְּאוּ עֲנִיֵּי־אָרֶץ׃ ענוי ק׳
5 הֵן פְּרָאִים ׀ בַּמִּדְבָּר
יָצְאוּ בְּפָעֳלָם מְשַׁחֲרֵי לַטָּרֶף
עֲרָבָה לוֹ לֶחֶם לַנְּעָרִים׃
6 בַּשָּׂדֶה בְּלִילוֹ יִקְצִירוּ יקצורו ק׳
וְכֶרֶם רָשָׁע יְלַקֵּשׁוּ׃
7 עָרוֹם יָלִינוּ מִבְּלִי לְבוּשׁ
וְאֵין כְּסוּת בַּקָּרָה׃
8 מִזֶּרֶם הָרִים יִרְטָבוּ
וּמִבְּלִי מַחְסֶה חִבְּקוּ־צוּר׃
9 יִגְזְלוּ מִשֹּׁד יָתוֹם
וְעַל־עָנִי יַחְבֹּלוּ׃
10 עָרוֹם הִלְּכוּ בְּלִי לְבוּשׁ
וּרְעֵבִים נָשְׂאוּ עֹמֶר׃
11 בֵּין־שׁוּרֹתָם יַצְהִירוּ
יְקָבִים דָּרְכוּ וַיִּצְמָאוּ׃
12 מֵעִיר מְתִים ׀ יִנְאָקוּ
וְנֶפֶשׁ־חֲלָלִים תְּשַׁוֵּעַ
וֶאֱלוֹהַּ לֹא־יָשִׂים תִּפְלָה׃

13 הֵמָּה ׀ הָיוּ בְּמֹרְדֵי־אוֹר
לֹא־הִכִּירוּ דְרָכָיו

Whatever He desires, He does.
14 For He will bring my term to an end,
But He has many more such at His disposal.
15 Therefore I am terrified at His presence;
When I consider, I dread Him.
16 God has made me fainthearted;
Shaddai has terrified me.
17 Yet I am not cut off by the darkness;
He has concealed the thick gloom from me.

24

Why are times for judgment not reserved by Shaddai?
Even those close to Him cannot foresee His actions.[a]
2 People remove boundary-stones;
They carry off flocks and pasture them;
3 They lead away the donkeys of the fatherless,
And seize the widow's bull as a pledge;
4 They chase the needy off the roads;
All the poor of the land are forced into hiding.
5 Like the wild asses of the wilderness,
They go about their tasks, seeking food;
The wilderness provides each with food for his lads;
6 They harvest fodder in the field,
And glean the late grapes in the vineyards of the wicked.
7 They pass the night naked for lack of clothing,
They have no covering against the cold;
8 They are drenched by the mountain rains,
And huddle against the rock for lack of shelter.
9 [b] They snatch the fatherless infant from the breast,
And seize the child of the poor as a pledge.
10 They go about naked for lack of clothing,
And, hungry, carry sheaves;
11 Between rows [of olive trees] they make oil,
And, thirsty, they tread the winepresses.
12 Men groan in the city;
The souls of the dying cry out;
Yet God does not regard it as a reproach.

13 They are rebels against the light;
They are strangers to its ways,

[a] *Lit. "days."*
[b] *This verse belongs to the description of the wicked in vv. 2–4a.*

וְלֹא יָשְׁבוּ בִּנְתִיבֹתָיו׃
14 לָאוֹר ׀ יָקוּם רוֹצֵחַ
יִקְטָל־עָנִי וְאֶבְיוֹן
וּבַלַּיְלָה יְהִי כַגַּנָּב׃
15 וְעֵין נֹאֵף ׀ שָׁמְרָה נֶשֶׁף
לֵאמֹר לֹא־תְשׁוּרֵנִי עָיִן
וְסֵתֶר פָּנִים יָשִׂים׃
16 חָתַר בַּחֹשֶׁךְ בָּתִּים
יוֹמָם חִתְּמוּ־לָמוֹ
לֹא־יָדְעוּ אוֹר׃
17 כִּי יַחְדָּו ׀ בֹּקֶר לָמוֹ צַלְמָוֶת
כִּי יַכִּיר בַּלְהוֹת צַלְמָוֶת׃
18 קַל־הוּא ׀ עַל־פְּנֵי־מַיִם
תְּקֻלַּל חֶלְקָתָם בָּאָרֶץ
לֹא־יִפְנֶה דֶּרֶךְ כְּרָמִים׃
19 צִיָּה גַם־חֹם יִגְזְלוּ מֵימֵי־שֶׁלֶג
שְׁאוֹל חָטָאוּ׃
20 יִשְׁכָּחֵהוּ רֶחֶם ׀ מְתָקוֹ רִמָּה
עוֹד לֹא־יִזָּכֵר
וַתִּשָּׁבֵר כָּעֵץ עַוְלָה׃
21 רֹעֶה עֲקָרָה לֹא תֵלֵד
וְאַלְמָנָה לֹא יְיֵטִיב׃
22 וּמָשַׁךְ אַבִּירִים בְּכֹחוֹ
יָקוּם וְלֹא־יַאֲמִין בַּחַיִּין׃
23 יִתֶּן־לוֹ לָבֶטַח וְיִשָּׁעֵן
וְעֵינֵיהוּ עַל־דַּרְכֵיהֶם׃
24 רֹמּוּ מְּעַט ׀ וְאֵינֶנּוּ נ״א רומו
וְהֻמְּכוּ כַּכֹּל יִקָּפְצוּן
וּכְרֹאשׁ שִׁבֹּלֶת יִמָּלוּ׃
25 וְאִם־לֹא אֵפוֹ מִי יַכְזִיבֵנִי
וְיָשֵׂם לְאַל מִלָּתִי׃

כה
1 וַיַּעַן בִּלְדַּד הַשֻּׁחִי וַיֹּאמַר׃

2 הַמְשֵׁל וָפַחַד עִמּוֹ
עֹשֶׂה שָׁלוֹם בִּמְרוֹמָיו׃

And do not stay in its path.
14 The murderer arises [c]in the evening[c]
To kill the poor and needy,
And at night he acts the thief.
15 The eyes of the adulterer watch for twilight,
Thinking, "No one will glimpse me then."
He masks his face.
16 In the dark they break into houses;
By day they shut themselves in;
They do not know the light.
17 For all of them morning is darkness;
It is then that they discern the terror of darkness.
18 [d] May they be flotsam on the face of the water;
May their portion in the land be cursed;
May none turn aside by way of their vineyards.
19 May drought and heat snatch away their snow waters,
And Sheol, those who have sinned.
20 May the womb forget him;
May he be sweet to the worms;
May he be no longer remembered;
May wrongdoers be broken like a tree.
21 May he consort with a barren woman who bears no child,
Leave his widow deprived of good.
22 Though he has the strength to seize bulls,
May he live with no assurance of survival.
23 Yet [God] gives him the security on which he relies,
And keeps watch over his affairs.
24 Exalted for a while, let them be gone;
Be brought low, and shrivel like mallows,
And wither like the heads of grain.

25 Surely no one can confute me,
Or prove that I am wrong.

25 Bildad the Shuhite said in reply:

2 Dominion and dread are His;
He imposes peace in His heights.

c-c *Cf. Mishnaic Heb.* 'or, *Aramaic* 'orta, *"evening"; others "with the light."*
d *From here to the end of the chapter the translation is largely conjectural.*

3 הֲיֵשׁ מִסְפָּר לִגְדוּדָיו
וְעַל־מִי לֹא־יָקוּם אוֹרֵהוּ׃
4 וּמַה־יִּצְדַּק אֱנוֹשׁ עִם־אֵל
וּמַה־יִּזְכֶּה יְלוּד אִשָּׁה׃
5 הֵן עַד־יָרֵחַ וְלֹא יַאֲהִיל
וְכוֹכָבִים לֹא־זַכּוּ בְעֵינָיו׃
6 אַף כִּי־אֱנוֹשׁ רִמָּה
וּבֶן־אָדָם תּוֹלֵעָה׃

כו
1 וַיַּעַן אִיּוֹב וַיֹּאמַר׃

2 מֶה־עָזַרְתָּ לְלֹא־כֹחַ
הוֹשַׁעְתָּ זְרוֹעַ לֹא־עֹז׃
3 מַה־יָּעַצְתָּ לְלֹא חָכְמָה
וְתֻשִׁיָּה לָרֹב הוֹדָעְתָּ׃
4 אֶת־מִי הִגַּדְתָּ מִלִּין
וְנִשְׁמַת־מִי יָצְאָה מִמֶּךָּ׃

5 הָרְפָאִים יְחוֹלָלוּ
מִתַּחַת מַיִם וְשֹׁכְנֵיהֶם׃
6 עָרוֹם שְׁאוֹל נֶגְדּוֹ
וְאֵין כְּסוּת לָאֲבַדּוֹן׃
7 נֹטֶה צָפוֹן עַל־תֹּהוּ
תֹּלֶה אֶרֶץ עַל־בְּלִימָה׃
8 צֹרֵר־מַיִם בְּעָבָיו
וְלֹא־נִבְקַע עָנָן תַּחְתָּם׃
9 מְאַחֵז פְּנֵי־כִסֵּה ה׳ במקום א׳
פַּרְשֵׁז עָלָיו עֲנָנוֹ׃
10 חֹק־חָג עַל־פְּנֵי־מָיִם
עַד־תַּכְלִית אוֹר עִם־חֹשֶׁךְ׃
11 עַמּוּדֵי שָׁמַיִם יְרוֹפָפוּ
וְיִתְמְהוּ מִגַּעֲרָתוֹ׃
12 בְּכֹחוֹ רָגַע הַיָּם
וּבִתוּבְנָתוֹ מָחַץ רָהַב׃ ובתבונתו ק׳
13 בְּרוּחוֹ שָׁמַיִם שִׁפְרָה
חֹלְלָה יָדוֹ נָחָשׁ בָּרִחַ׃
14 הֶן־אֵלֶּה ׀ קְצוֹת דְּרָכָו דרכיו ק׳
וּמַה־שֵּׁמֶץ דָּבָר נִשְׁמַע־בּוֹ
וְרַעַם גְּבוּרֹתָו מִי יִתְבּוֹנָן׃ גבורתיו ק

3 Can His troops be numbered?
On whom does His light not shine?
4 How can man be in the right before God?
How can one born of woman be cleared of guilt?
5 Even the moon is not bright,
And the stars are not pure in His sight.
6 How much less man, a worm,
The son-of-man, a maggot.

26

1 Then Job said in reply:

2 You would help without having the strength;
You would deliver with arms that have no power.
3 Without having the wisdom, you offer advice
And freely give your counsel.
4 To whom have you addressed words?
Whose breath issued from you?

5 The shades tremble
Beneath the waters and their denizens.
6 Sheol is naked before Him;
Abaddon has no cover.
7 He it is who stretched out Zaphon[a] over chaos,
Who suspended earth over emptiness.
8 He wrapped up the waters in His clouds;
Yet no cloud burst under its weight.
9 [b]He shuts off the view of His throne,
Spreading His cloud over it.[b]
10 He drew a boundary on the surface of the waters,
At the extreme where light and darkness meet.
11 The pillars of heaven tremble,
Astounded at His blast.
12 By His power He stilled the sea;
By His skill He struck down Rahab.
13 By His wind the heavens were calmed;
His hand pierced the [c]Elusive Serpent.[c]
14 These are but glimpses of His rule,
The mere whisper that we perceive of Him;
Who can absorb the thunder of His mighty deeds?

a *Used for heaven; cf. Ps. 48.3.*
b-b *Meaning of Heb. uncertain.*
c-c *Cf. Isa. 27.1.*

כז

1 וַיֹּסֶף אִיּוֹב שְׂאֵת מְשָׁלוֹ וַיֹּאמַר׃

2 חַי־אֵל הֵסִיר מִשְׁפָּטִי
וְשַׁדַּי הֵמַר נַפְשִׁי׃
3 כִּי־כָל־עוֹד נִשְׁמָתִי בִי
וְרוּחַ אֱלוֹהַּ בְּאַפִּי׃
4 אִם־תְּדַבֵּרְנָה שְׂפָתַי עַוְלָה
וּלְשׁוֹנִי אִם־יֶהְגֶּה רְמִיָּה׃
5 חָלִילָה לִּי אִם־אַצְדִּיק אֶתְכֶם
עַד־אֶגְוָע לֹא־אָסִיר תֻּמָּתִי מִמֶּנִּי׃
6 בְּצִדְקָתִי הֶחֱזַקְתִּי וְלֹא אַרְפֶּהָ
לֹא־יֶחֱרַף לְבָבִי מִיָּמָי׃

7 יְהִי כְרָשָׁע אֹיְבִי
וּמִתְקוֹמְמִי כְעַוָּל׃
8 כִּי מַה־תִּקְוַת חָנֵף כִּי יִבְצָע
כִּי יֵשֶׁל אֱלוֹהַּ נַפְשׁוֹ׃
9 הֲצַעֲקָתוֹ יִשְׁמַע ׀ אֵל
כִּי־תָבוֹא עָלָיו צָרָה׃
10 אִם־עַל־שַׁדַּי יִתְעַנָּג
יִקְרָא אֱלוֹהַּ בְּכָל־עֵת׃
11 אוֹרֶה אֶתְכֶם בְּיַד־אֵל
אֲשֶׁר עִם־שַׁדַּי לֹא אֲכַחֵד׃
12 הֵן אַתֶּם כֻּלְּכֶם חֲזִיתֶם
וְלָמָּה־זֶּה הֶבֶל תֶּהְבָּלוּ׃
13 זֶה ׀ חֵלֶק־אָדָם רָשָׁע ׀ עִם־אֵל
וְנַחֲלַת עָרִיצִים מִשַּׁדַּי יִקָּחוּ׃
14 אִם־יִרְבּוּ בָנָיו לְמוֹ־חָרֶב
וְצֶאֱצָאָיו לֹא יִשְׂבְּעוּ־לָחֶם׃

15 שְׂרִידָיו בַּמָּוֶת יִקָּבֵרוּ
וְאַלְמְנֹתָיו לֹא תִבְכֶּינָה׃
16 אִם־יִצְבֹּר כֶּעָפָר כָּסֶף
וְכַחֹמֶר יָכִין מַלְבּוּשׁ׃
17 יָכִין וְצַדִּיק יִלְבָּשׁ
וְכֶסֶף נָקִי יַחֲלֹק׃
18 בָּנָה כָעָשׁ בֵּיתוֹ
וּכְסֻכָּה עָשָׂה נֹצֵר׃
19 עָשִׁיר יִשְׁכַּב וְלֹא יֵאָסֵף
עֵינָיו פָּקַח וְאֵינֶנּוּ׃

27

Job again took up his theme and said:

2 By God who deprived me of justice!
By Shaddai who has embittered my life!
3 As long as there is life in me,
And God's breath is in my nostrils,
4 My lips will speak no wrong,
Nor my tongue utter deceit.
5 Far be it from me to say you are right;
Until I die I will maintain my integrity.
6 I persist in my righteousness and will not yield;
[a]I shall be free of reproach[a] as long as I live.

7 May my enemy be as the wicked;
My assailant, as the wrongdoer.
8 For what hope has the impious man when he is cut down,
When God takes away his life?
9 Will God hear his cry
When trouble comes upon him,
10 When he seeks the favor of Shaddai,
Calls upon God at all times?
11 I will teach you what is in God's power,
And what is with Shaddai I will not conceal.
12 All of you have seen it,
So why talk nonsense?
13 This is the evil man's portion from God,
The lot that the ruthless receive from Shaddai:
14 Should he have many sons—they are marked for the sword;
His descendants will never have their fill of bread;
15 Those who survive him will be buried in a plague,
And their widows will not weep;
16 Should he pile up silver like dust,
Lay up clothing like dirt—
17 He may lay it up, but the righteous will wear it,
And the innocent will share the silver.
18 The house he built is like a bird's nest,
Like the booth a watchman makes.
19 He lies down, a rich man, with [his wealth] intact;
When he opens his eyes it will be gone.

a-a *Meaning of Heb. uncertain.*

20 תַּשִּׂיגֵהוּ כַמַּיִם בַּלָּהוֹת	20 Terror will overtake him like a flood;
לַיְלָה גְּנָבַתּוּ סוּפָה׃	A storm wind will make off with him by night.
21 יִשָּׂאֵהוּ קָדִים וְיֵלַךְ פתח באתנח	21 The east wind carries him far away, and he is gone;
וִישָׂעֲרֵהוּ מִמְּקֹמוֹ׃	It sweeps him from his place.
22 וְיַשְׁלֵךְ עָלָיו וְלֹא יַחְמֹל	22 Then it hurls itself at him without mercy;
מִיָּדוֹ בָּרוֹחַ יִבְרָח׃	He tries to escape from its force.
23 יִשְׂפֹּק עָלֵימוֹ כַפֵּימוֹ	23 It claps its hands at him,
וְיִשְׁרֹק עָלָיו מִמְּקֹמוֹ׃	And whistles at him from its place.
כח	28
1 כִּי יֵשׁ לַכֶּסֶף מוֹצָא	There is a mine for silver,
וּמָקוֹם לַזָּהָב יָזֹקּוּ׃	And a place where gold is refined.
2 בַּרְזֶל מֵעָפָר יֻקָּח	2 Iron is taken out of the earth,
וְאֶבֶן יָצוּק נְחוּשָׁה׃	And copper smelted from rock.
3 קֵץ ׀ שָׂם לַחֹשֶׁךְ	3 He sets bounds for darkness;
וּלְכָל־תַּכְלִית הוּא חוֹקֵר	To every limit man probes,
אֶבֶן אֹפֶל וְצַלְמָוֶת׃	To rocks in deepest darkness.
4 פָּרַץ נַחַל ׀ מֵעִם־גָּר	4 [a]-They open up a shaft far from where men live,
הַנִּשְׁכָּחִים מִנִּי־רָגֶל	[In places] forgotten by wayfarers,
דַּלּוּ מֵאֱנוֹשׁ נָעוּ׃	Destitute of men, far removed.-[a]
5 אֶרֶץ מִמֶּנָּה יֵצֵא־לָחֶם	5 Earth, out of which food grows,
וְתַחְתֶּיהָ נֶהְפַּךְ כְּמוֹ־אֵשׁ׃	Is changed below as if into fire.
6 מְקוֹם־סַפִּיר אֲבָנֶיהָ	6 Its rocks are a place of sapphires;
וְעַפְרֹת זָהָב לוֹ׃	It contains gold dust too.
7 נָתִיב לֹא־יְדָעוֹ עָיִט	7 No bird of prey knows the path to it;
וְלֹא שְׁזָפַתּוּ עֵין אַיָּה׃	The falcon's eye has not gazed upon it.
8 לֹא־הִדְרִיכֻהוּ בְנֵי־שָׁחַץ	8 The proud beasts have not reached it;
לֹא־עָדָה עָלָיו שָׁחַל׃	The lion has not crossed it.
9 בַּחַלָּמִישׁ שָׁלַח יָדוֹ	9 Man sets his hand against the flinty rock
הָפַךְ מִשֹּׁרֶשׁ הָרִים׃	And overturns mountains by the roots.
10 בַּצּוּרוֹת יְאֹרִים בִּקֵּעַ	10 He carves out channels through rock;
וְכָל־יְקָר רָאֲתָה עֵינוֹ׃	His eyes behold every precious thing.
11 מִבְּכִי נְהָרוֹת חִבֵּשׁ	11 He dams up the sources of the streams
וְתַעֲלֻמָהּ יֹצִא אוֹר׃	So that hidden things may be brought to light.
12 וְהַחָכְמָה מֵאַיִן תִּמָּצֵא	12 But where can wisdom be found;
וְאֵי־זֶה מְקוֹם בִּינָה׃	Where is the place of understanding?
13 לֹא־יָדַע אֱנוֹשׁ עֶרְכָּהּ	13 No man can set a value on it;
וְלֹא תִמָּצֵא בְּאֶרֶץ הַחַיִּים׃	It cannot be found in the land of the living.
14 תְּהוֹם אָמַר לֹא בִי־הִיא	14 The Deep says, "It is not in me";
וְיָם אָמַר אֵין עִמָּדִי׃	The Sea says, "I do not have it."

a-a *Meaning of Heb. uncertain.*

15 לֹא־יֻתַּן סְגוֹר תַּחְתֶּיהָ
וְלֹא יִשָּׁקֵל כֶּסֶף מְחִירָהּ׃
16 לֹא תְסֻלֶּה בְּכֶתֶם אוֹפִיר
בְּשֹׁהַם יָקָר וְסַפִּיר׃
17 לֹא־יַעַרְכֶנָּה זָהָב וּזְכוֹכִית
וּתְמוּרָתָהּ כְּלִי־פָז׃
18 רָאמוֹת וְגָבִישׁ לֹא יִזָּכֵר
וּמֶשֶׁךְ חָכְמָה מִפְּנִינִים׃
19 לֹא־יַעַרְכֶנָּה פִּטְדַת־כּוּשׁ
בְּכֶתֶם טָהוֹר לֹא תְסֻלֶּה׃

20 וְהַחָכְמָה מֵאַיִן תָּבוֹא
וְאֵי־זֶה מְקוֹם בִּינָה׃
21 וְנֶעֶלְמָה מֵעֵינֵי כָל־חָי
וּמֵעוֹף הַשָּׁמַיִם נִסְתָּרָה׃
22 אֲבַדּוֹן וָמָוֶת אָמְרוּ
בְּאָזְנֵינוּ שָׁמַעְנוּ שִׁמְעָהּ׃
23 אֱלֹהִים הֵבִין דַּרְכָּהּ
וְהוּא יָדַע אֶת־מְקוֹמָהּ׃
24 כִּי־הוּא לִקְצוֹת־הָאָרֶץ יַבִּיט
תַּחַת כָּל־הַשָּׁמַיִם יִרְאֶה׃
25 לַעֲשׂוֹת לָרוּחַ מִשְׁקָל
וּמַיִם תִּכֵּן בְּמִדָּה׃
26 בַּעֲשֹׂתוֹ לַמָּטָר חֹק
וְדֶרֶךְ לַחֲזִיז קֹלוֹת׃
27 אָז רָאָהּ וַיְסַפְּרָהּ
הֱכִינָהּ וְגַם־חֲקָרָהּ׃
28 וַיֹּאמֶר ׀ לָאָדָם
הֵן יִרְאַת אֲדֹנָי הִיא חָכְמָה
וְסוּר מֵרָע בִּינָה׃

15 It cannot be bartered for gold;
Silver cannot be paid out as its price.
16 The finest gold of Ophir cannot be weighed against it,
Nor precious onyx, nor sapphire.
17 Gold or glass cannot match its value,
Nor vessels of fine gold be exchanged for it.
18 Coral and crystal cannot be mentioned with it;
A pouch of wisdom is better than rubies.
19 Topaz from Nubia cannot match its value;
Pure gold cannot be weighed against it.

20 But whence does wisdom come?
Where is the place of understanding?
21 It is hidden from the eyes of all living,
Concealed from the fowl of heaven.
22 Abaddon and Death say,
"We have only a report of it."
23 God understands the way to it;
He knows its place;
24 For He sees to the ends of the earth,
Observes all that is beneath the heavens.
25 When He fixed the weight of the winds,
Set the measure of the waters;
26 When He made a rule for the rain
And a course for the thunderstorms,
27 Then He saw it and gauged it;
He measured it and probed it.
28 He said to man,
"See! Fear of the Lord is wisdom;
To shun evil is understanding."

כט

1 וַיֹּסֶף אִיּוֹב שְׂאֵת מְשָׁלוֹ וַיֹּאמַר׃

2 מִי־יִתְּנֵנִי כְיַרְחֵי־קֶדֶם
כִּימֵי אֱלוֹהַּ יִשְׁמְרֵנִי׃
3 בְּהִלּוֹ נֵרוֹ עֲלֵי רֹאשִׁי
לְאוֹרוֹ אֵלֶךְ חֹשֶׁךְ׃
4 כַּאֲשֶׁר הָיִיתִי בִּימֵי חָרְפִּי
בְּסוֹד אֱלוֹהַּ עֲלֵי אָהֳלִי׃
5 בְּעוֹד שַׁדַּי עִמָּדִי
סְבִיבוֹתַי נְעָרָי׃

29

Job again took up his theme and said:

2 O that I were as in months gone by,
In the days when God watched over me,
3 When His lamp shone over my head,
When I walked in the dark by its light,
4 When I was in my prime,
When God's company graced my tent,
5 When Shaddai was still with me,
When my lads surrounded me,

6 בִּרְחֹץ הֲלִיכַי בְּחֵמָה
וְצוּר יָצוּק עִמָּדִי פַּלְגֵי־שָׁמֶן׃
7 בְּצֵאתִי שַׁעַר עֲלֵי־קָרֶת
בָּרְחוֹב אָכִין מוֹשָׁבִי׃
8 רָאוּנִי נְעָרִים וְנֶחְבָּאוּ
וִישִׁישִׁים קָמוּ עָמָדוּ׃
9 שָׂרִים עָצְרוּ בְמִלִּים
וְכַף יָשִׂימוּ לְפִיהֶם׃
10 קוֹל־נְגִידִים נֶחְבָּאוּ
וּלְשׁוֹנָם לְחִכָּם דָּבֵקָה׃
11 כִּי אֹזֶן שָׁמְעָה וַתְּאַשְּׁרֵנִי
וְעַיִן רָאֲתָה וַתְּעִידֵנִי׃
12 כִּי־אֲמַלֵּט עָנִי מְשַׁוֵּעַ
וְיָתוֹם וְלֹא־עֹזֵר לוֹ׃
13 בִּרְכַּת אֹבֵד עָלַי תָּבֹא
וְלֵב אַלְמָנָה אַרְנִן׃
14 צֶדֶק לָבַשְׁתִּי וַיִּלְבָּשֵׁנִי
כִּמְעִיל וְצָנִיף מִשְׁפָּטִי׃
15 עֵינַיִם הָיִיתִי לַעִוֵּר
וְרַגְלַיִם לַפִּסֵּחַ אָנִי׃
16 אָב אָנֹכִי לָאֶבְיוֹנִים
וְרִב לֹא־יָדַעְתִּי אֶחְקְרֵהוּ׃
17 וָאֲשַׁבְּרָה מְתַלְּעוֹת עַוָּל
וּמִשִּׁנָּיו אַשְׁלִיךְ טָרֶף׃
18 וָאֹמַר עִם־קִנִּי אֶגְוָע
וְכַחוֹל אַרְבֶּה יָמִים׃ לנהרדעי וכחול בשורק
19 שָׁרְשִׁי פָתוּחַ אֱלֵי־מָיִם
וְטַל יָלִין בִּקְצִירִי׃
20 כְּבוֹדִי חָדָשׁ עִמָּדִי
וְקַשְׁתִּי בְּיָדִי תַחֲלִיף׃
21 לִי־שָׁמְעוּ וְיִחֵלּוּ
וְיִדְּמוּ לְמוֹ עֲצָתִי׃
22 אַחֲרֵי דְבָרִי לֹא יִשְׁנוּ
וְעָלֵימוֹ תִּטֹּף מִלָּתִי׃
23 וְיִחֲלוּ כַמָּטָר לִי
וּפִיהֶם פָּעֲרוּ לְמַלְקוֹשׁ׃
24 אֶשְׂחַק אֲלֵהֶם לֹא יַאֲמִינוּ
וְאוֹר פָּנַי לֹא יַפִּילוּן׃
25 אֶבְחַר דַּרְכָּם וְאֵשֵׁב רֹאשׁ

6 When my feet were bathed in cream,
And rocks poured out streams of oil for me.
7 When I passed through the city gates
To take my seat in the square,
8 Young men saw me and hid,
Elders rose and stood;
9 Nobles held back their words;
They clapped their hands to their mouths.
10 The voices of princes were hushed;
Their tongues stuck to their palates.
11 The ear that heard me acclaimed me;
The eye that saw, commended me.
12 For I saved the poor man who cried out,
The orphan who had none to help him.
13 I received the blessing of the wretched;
I gladdened the heart of the widow.
14 I clothed myself in righteousness and it robed me;
Justice was my cloak and turban.
15 I was eyes to the blind
And feet to the lame.
16 I was a father to the needy,
And I looked into the case of the stranger.
17 I broke the jaws of the wrongdoer,
And I wrested prey from his teeth.
18 I thought I would end my days with my family,[a]
And [b]be as long-lived as the phoenix,[b]
19 My roots reaching water,
And dew lying on my branches;
20 My vigor refreshed,
My bow ever new in my hand.
21 Men would listen to me expectantly,
And wait for my counsel.
22 After I spoke they had nothing to say;
My words were as drops [of dew] upon them.
23 They waited for me as for rain,
For the late rain, their mouths open wide.
24 When I smiled at them, they would not believe it;
They never expected[c] a sign of my favor.
25 I decided their course and presided over them;

[a] *Lit. "nest."*
[b-b] *Others "multiply days like sand."*
[c] *Taking* yappilun *as from* pll; *cf. Gen. 48.11.*

וְאֶשְׁכּוֹן כְּמֶלֶךְ בַּגְּדוּד
כַּאֲשֶׁר אֲבֵלִים יְנַחֵם׃

ל

1 וְעַתָּה ׀ שָׂחֲקוּ עָלַי
צְעִירִים מִמֶּנִּי לְיָמִים
אֲשֶׁר־מָאַסְתִּי אֲבוֹתָם
לָשִׁית עִם־כַּלְבֵי צֹאנִי׃
2 גַּם־כֹּחַ יְדֵיהֶם לָמָּה לִּי
עָלֵימוֹ אָבַד כָּלַח׃
3 בְּחֶסֶר וּבְכָפָן גַּלְמוּד
הַעֹרְקִים צִיָּה
אֶמֶשׁ שׁוֹאָה וּמְשֹׁאָה׃
4 הַקֹּטְפִים מַלּוּחַ עֲלֵי־שִׂיחַ
וְשֹׁרֶשׁ רְתָמִים לַחְמָם׃
5 מִן־גֵּו יְגֹרָשׁוּ
יָרִיעוּ עָלֵימוֹ כַּגַּנָּב׃
6 בַּעֲרוּץ נְחָלִים לִשְׁכֹּן
חֹרֵי עָפָר וְכֵפִים׃
7 בֵּין־שִׂיחִים יִנְהָקוּ
תַּחַת חָרוּל יְסֻפָּחוּ׃
8 בְּנֵי־נָבָל גַּם־בְּנֵי בְלִי־שֵׁם
נִכְּאוּ מִן־הָאָרֶץ׃

9 וְעַתָּה נְגִינָתָם הָיִיתִי
וָאֱהִי לָהֶם לְמִלָּה׃
10 תִּעֲבוּנִי רָחֲקוּ מֶנִּי
וּמִפָּנַי לֹא־חָשְׂכוּ רֹק׃
11 כִּי־יתרו פִתַּח וַיְעַנֵּנִי (יתרי ק׳)
וְרֶסֶן מִפָּנַי שִׁלֵּחוּ׃
12 עַל־יָמִין פִּרְחַח יָקוּמוּ
רַגְלַי שִׁלֵּחוּ
וַיָּסֹלּוּ עָלַי אָרְחוֹת אֵידָם׃
13 נָתְסוּ נְתִיבָתִי
לְהַוָּתִי יֹעִילוּ לֹא עֹזֵר לָמוֹ׃ (להותי ק׳)

14 כְּפֶרֶץ רָחָב יֶאֱתָיוּ
תַּחַת שֹׁאָה הִתְגַּלְגָּלוּ׃
15 הָהְפַּךְ עָלַי בַּלָּהוֹת
תִּרְדֹּף כָּרוּחַ נְדִבָתִי

I lived like a king among his troops,
Like one who consoles mourners.

30

But now those younger than I deride me,
[Men] whose fathers I would have disdained to put among
my sheep dogs.
2 What need have I of their strong hands?
All their vigor[a] is gone.
3 Wasted from want and starvation,
They flee to a parched land,
To the gloom of desolate wasteland.
4 They pluck saltwort and wormwood;
The roots of broom are their food.
5 Driven out [a]from society,[a]
They are cried at like a thief.
6 They live in the gullies of wadis,
In holes in the ground, and in rocks,
7 Braying among the bushes,
Huddling among the nettles,
8 Scoundrels, nobodies,
Stricken from the earth.

9 Now I am the butt of their gibes;
I have become a byword to them.
10 They abhor me; they keep their distance from me;
They do not withhold spittle from my face.
11 Because God[b] has disarmed[c] and humbled me,
They have thrown off restraint in my presence.
12 Mere striplings assail me at my right hand:
They put me to flight;
They build their roads for my ruin.
13 They tear up my path;
They promote my fall,
Although it does them no good.
14 They come as through a wide breach;
They roll in [a]like raging billows.[a]
15 Terror tumbles upon me;
It sweeps away my honor like the wind;

[a] *Meaning of Heb. uncertain.*
[b] *Lit. "He."*
[c] *Lit. "loosened my [bow] string."*

וּכְעָב עָבְרָה יְשֻׁעָתִי׃	My dignity[d] vanishes like a cloud.
16 וְעַתָּה עָלַי תִּשְׁתַּפֵּךְ נַפְשִׁי	16 So now my life runs out;
יֹאחֲזוּנִי יְמֵי־עֹנִי׃	Days of misery have taken hold of me.
17 לַיְלָה עֲצָמַי נִקַּר מֵעָלָי	17 By night my bones feel gnawed;
וְעֹרְקַי לֹא יִשְׁכָּבוּן׃	My sinews never rest.
18 בְּרָב־כֹּחַ יִתְחַפֵּשׂ לְבוּשִׁי	18 [a]-With great effort I change clothing;
כְּפִי כֻתָּנְתִּי יַאַזְרֵנִי׃	The neck of my tunic fits my waist.-[a]
19 הֹרָנִי לַחֹמֶר	19 He regarded me as clay,
וָאֶתְמַשֵּׁל כֶּעָפָר וָאֵפֶר׃	I have become like dust and ashes.
20 אֲשַׁוַּע אֵלֶיךָ וְלֹא תַעֲנֵנִי	20 I cry out to You, but You do not answer me;
עָמַדְתִּי וַתִּתְבֹּנֶן בִּי׃	I wait, but You do [not] consider me.
21 תֵּהָפֵךְ לְאַכְזָר לִי	21 You have become cruel to me;
בְּעֹצֶם יָדְךָ תִשְׂטְמֵנִי׃	With Your powerful hand You harass me.
22 תִּשָּׂאֵנִי אֶל־רוּחַ תַּרְכִּיבֵנִי	22 You lift me up and mount me on the wind;
וּתְמֹגְגֵנִי תְּשֻׁוָּה׃ תשיה ק׳	You make my courage melt.
23 כִּי־יָדַעְתִּי מָוֶת תְּשִׁיבֵנִי	23 I know You will bring me to death,
וּבֵית מוֹעֵד לְכָל־חָי׃	The house assigned for all the living.
24 אַךְ לֹא־בְעִי יִשְׁלַח־יָד	24 [a]-Surely He would not strike at a ruin
אִם־בְּפִידוֹ לָהֶן שׁוּעַ׃	If, in calamity, one cried out to Him.-[a]
25 אִם־לֹא בָכִיתִי לִקְשֵׁה־יוֹם	25 Did I not weep for the unfortunate?
עָגְמָה נַפְשִׁי לָאֶבְיוֹן׃	Did I not grieve for the needy?
26 כִּי טוֹב קִוִּיתִי וַיָּבֹא רָע	26 I looked forward to good fortune, but evil came;
וַאֲיַחֲלָה לְאוֹר וַיָּבֹא אֹפֶל׃	I hoped for light, but darkness came.
27 מֵעַי רֻתְּחוּ וְלֹא־דָמּוּ	27 My bowels are in turmoil without respite;
קִדְּמֻנִי יְמֵי־עֹנִי׃	Days of misery confront me.
28 קֹדֵר הִלַּכְתִּי בְּלֹא חַמָּה	28 I walk about in sunless gloom;
קַמְתִּי בַקָּהָל אֲשַׁוֵּעַ׃	I rise in the assembly and cry out.
29 אָח הָיִיתִי לְתַנִּים	29 I have become a brother to jackals,
וְרֵעַ לִבְנוֹת יַעֲנָה׃	A companion to ostriches.
30 עוֹרִי שָׁחַר מֵעָלָי	30 My skin, blackened, is peeling off me;
וְעַצְמִי־חָרָה מִנִּי־חֹרֶב׃	My bones are charred by the heat.
31 וַיְהִי לְאֵבֶל כִּנֹּרִי	31 So my lyre is given over to mourning,
וְעֻגָבִי לְקוֹל בֹּכִים׃ בנ״א הג׳ דגושה	My pipe, to accompany weepers.

לא

31

1 בְּרִית כָּרַתִּי לְעֵינָי	I have covenanted with my eyes
וּמָה אֶתְבּוֹנֵן עַל־בְּתוּלָה׃	Not to gaze on a maiden.
2 וּמֶה ׀ חֵלֶק אֱלוֹהַּ מִמָּעַל	2 What fate is decreed by God above?
וְנַחֲלַת שַׁדַּי מִמְּרֹמִים׃	What lot, by Shaddai in the heights?
3 הֲלֹא־אֵיד לְעַוָּל	3 Calamity is surely for the iniquitous;

[d] *Heb.* yeshu'athi *taken as related to* sho'a, *"noble."*

וְנֵכֶר לְפֹעֲלֵי אָוֶן׃
4 הֲלֹא־הוּא יִרְאֶה דְרָכָי
וְכָל־צְעָדַי יִסְפּוֹר׃

5 אִם־הָלַכְתִּי עִם־שָׁוְא
וַתַּחַשׁ עַל־מִרְמָה רַגְלִי׃
6 יִשְׁקְלֵנִי בְמֹאזְנֵי־צֶדֶק
וְיֵדַע אֱלוֹהַּ תֻּמָּתִי׃
7 אִם־תִּטֶּה אַשֻּׁרִי מִנִּי הַדָּרֶךְ
וְאַחַר עֵינַי הָלַךְ לִבִּי
וּבְכַפַּי דָּבַק מְאוּם׃ א׳ נחה
8 אֶזְרְעָה וְאַחֵר יֹאכֵל
וְצֶאֱצָאַי יְשֹׁרָשׁוּ׃
9 אִם־נִפְתָּה לִבִּי עַל־אִשָּׁה
וְעַל־פֶּתַח רֵעִי אָרָבְתִּי׃
10 תִּטְחַן לְאַחֵר אִשְׁתִּי
וְעָלֶיהָ יִכְרְעוּן אֲחֵרִין׃
11 כִּי־הוּא זִמָּה היא ק׳
וְהִיא עָוֺן פְּלִילִים׃ והוא ק׳ במקצת ספרים בלא מ׳
12 כִּי אֵשׁ הִיא עַד־אֲבַדּוֹן תֹּאכֵל
וּבְכָל־תְּבוּאָתִי תְשָׁרֵשׁ׃
13 אִם־אֶמְאַס מִשְׁפַּט עַבְדִּי וַאֲמָתִי
בְּרִבָם עִמָּדִי׃

14 וּמָה אֶעֱשֶׂה כִּי־יָקוּם אֵל
וְכִי־יִפְקֹד מָה אֲשִׁיבֶנּוּ׃
15 הֲלֹא־בַבֶּטֶן עֹשֵׂנִי עָשָׂהוּ
וַיְכֻנֶנּוּ בָּרֶחֶם אֶחָד׃

16 אִם־אֶמְנַע מֵחֵפֶץ דַּלִּים
וְעֵינֵי אַלְמָנָה אֲכַלֶּה׃
17 וְאֹכַל פִּתִּי לְבַדִּי
וְלֹא־אָכַל יָתוֹם מִמֶּנָּה׃
18 כִּי מִנְּעוּרַי גְּדֵלַנִי כְאָב
וּמִבֶּטֶן אִמִּי אַנְחֶנָּה׃

19 אִם־אֶרְאֶה אוֹבֵד מִבְּלִי לְבוּשׁ
וְאֵין כְּסוּת לָאֶבְיוֹן׃
20 אִם־לֹא בֵרְכוּנִי חֲלָצָו חלציו ק׳
וּמִגֵּז כְּבָשַׂי יִתְחַמָּם׃

Misfortune, for the worker of mischief.
4 Surely He observes my ways,
Takes account of my every step.

5 Have I walked with worthless men,
Or my feet hurried to deceit?
6 Let Him weigh me on the scale of righteousness;
Let God ascertain my integrity.
7 If my feet have strayed from their course,
My heart followed after my eyes,
And a stain sullied my hands,
8 May I sow, but another reap,
May the growth of my field be uprooted!
9 If my heart was ravished by the wife of my neighbor,
And I lay in wait at his door,
10 May my wife grind for another,
May others kneel over her!
11 For that would have been debauchery,
A criminal offense,
12 A fire burning down to Abaddon,
Consuming the roots of all my increase.
13 Did I ever brush aside the case of my servants, man or maid,
When they made a complaint against me?

14 What then should I do when God arises;
When He calls me to account, what should I answer Him?
15 Did not He who made me in my mother's belly make him?
Did not One form us both in the womb?

16 Did I deny the poor their needs,
Or let a[a] widow pine away,
17 By eating my food alone,
The fatherless not eating of it also?
18 Why, from my youth he grew up with me as though I were his father;
Since I left my mother's womb I was her[b] guide.

19 I never saw an unclad wretch,
A needy man without clothing,
20 Whose loins did not bless me
As he warmed himself with the shearings of my sheep.

[a] *Lit. "the eyes of a."*
[b] *Viz. the widow's.*

21 אִם־הֲנִפוֹתִי עַל־יָתוֹם יָדִי
כִּי־אֶרְאֶה בַשַּׁעַר עֶזְרָתִי׃
22 כְּתֵפִי מִשִּׁכְמָה תִפּוֹל
וְאֶזְרֹעִי מִקָּנָה תִשָּׁבֵר׃
23 כִּי־פַחַד אֵלַי אֵיד אֵל
וּמִשְּׂאֵתוֹ לֹא אוּכָל׃
24 אִם־שַׂמְתִּי זָהָב כִּסְלִי
וְלַכֶּתֶם אָמַרְתִּי מִבְטַחִי׃
25 אִם־אֶשְׂמַח כִּי־רַב חֵילִי
וְכִי־כַבִּיר מָצְאָה יָדִי׃
26 אִם־אֶרְאֶה אוֹר כִּי יָהֵל
וְיָרֵחַ יָקָר הֹלֵךְ׃
27 וַיִּפְתְּ בַּסֵּתֶר לִבִּי
וַתִּשַּׁק יָדִי לְפִי׃
28 גַּם־הוּא עָוֺן פְּלִילִי
כִּי־כִחַשְׁתִּי לָאֵל מִמָּעַל׃
29 אִם־אֶשְׂמַח בְּפִיד מְשַׂנְאִי
וְהִתְעֹרַרְתִּי כִּי־מְצָאוֹ רָע׃
30 וְלֹא־נָתַתִּי לַחֲטֹא חִכִּי
לִשְׁאֹל בְּאָלָה נַפְשׁוֹ׃
31 אִם־לֹא אָמְרוּ מְתֵי אָהֳלִי
מִי־יִתֵּן מִבְּשָׂרוֹ לֹא נִשְׂבָּע׃
32 בַּחוּץ לֹא־יָלִין גֵּר
דְּלָתַי לָאֹרַח אֶפְתָּח׃
33 אִם־כִּסִּיתִי כְאָדָם פְּשָׁעָי
לִטְמוֹן בְּחֻבִּי עֲוֺנִי׃
34 כִּי אֶעֱרוֹץ ׀ הָמוֹן רַבָּה
וּבוּז־מִשְׁפָּחוֹת יְחִתֵּנִי
וָאֶדֹּם לֹא־אֵצֵא פָתַח׃

35 מִי יִתֶּן־לִי ׀ שֹׁמֵעַ לִי
הֶן־תָּוִי שַׁדַּי יַעֲנֵנִי
וְסֵפֶר כָּתַב אִישׁ רִיבִי׃
36 אִם־לֹא עַל־שִׁכְמִי אֶשָּׂאֶנּוּ
אֶעֶנְדֶנּוּ עֲטָרוֹת לִי׃
37 מִסְפַּר צְעָדַי אַגִּידֶנּוּ
כְּמוֹ־נָגִיד אֲקָרְבֶנּוּ׃

38 אִם־עָלַי אַדְמָתִי תִזְעָק
וְיַחַד תְּלָמֶיהָ יִבְכָּיוּן׃

21 If I raised my hand against the fatherless,
Looking to my supporters in the gate,
22 May my arm drop off my shoulder;
My forearm break off [c]at the elbow.[c]
23 For I am in dread of God-sent calamity;
I cannot bear His threat.
24 Did I put my reliance on gold,
Or regard fine gold as my bulwark?
25 Did I rejoice in my great wealth,
In having attained plenty?
26 If ever I saw the light shining,
The moon on its course in full glory,
27 And I secretly succumbed,
And my hand touched my mouth in a kiss,
28 That, too, would have been a criminal offense,
For I would have denied God above.
29 Did I rejoice over my enemy's misfortune?
Did I thrill because evil befell him?
30 I never let my mouth[d] sin
By wishing his death in a curse.
31 (Indeed, the men of my clan said,
"We would consume his flesh insatiably!")
32 No sojourner spent the night in the open;
I opened my doors to the road.
33 Did I hide my transgressions like Adam,
Bury my wrongdoing in my bosom,
34 That I [now] fear the great multitude,
And am shattered by the contempt of families,
So that I keep silent and do not step outdoors?

35 O that I had someone to give me a hearing;
O that Shaddai would reply to my writ,
Or my accuser draw up a true bill!
36 I would carry it on my shoulder;
Tie it around me for a wreath.
37 I would give him an account of my steps,
Offer it as to a commander.

38 If my land cries out against me,
Its furrows weep together;

[c-c] *Lit. "from its shaft," i.e. the humerus.*
[d] *Lit. "palate."*

39 אִם־כֹּחָהּ אָכַלְתִּי בְלִי־כָסֶף
וְנֶפֶשׁ בְּעָלֶיהָ הִפָּחְתִּי׃
40 תַּחַת חִטָּה ׀ יֵצֵא חוֹחַ
וְתַחַת־שְׂעֹרָה בָאְשָׁה

תַּמּוּ דִּבְרֵי אִיּוֹב׃

[39] If I have eaten its produce without payment,
And made its [rightful] owners despair,
[40] May nettles grow there instead of wheat;
Instead of barley, stinkweed!

The words of Job are at an end.

לב

1 וַיִּשְׁבְּתוּ שְׁלֹשֶׁת הָאֲנָשִׁים הָאֵלֶּה
מֵעֲנוֹת אֶת־אִיּוֹב כִּי הוּא צַדִּיק
2 בְּעֵינָיו׃ וַיִּחַר אַף ׀ אֱלִיהוּא בֶן־
בַּרַכְאֵל הַבּוּזִי מִמִּשְׁפַּחַת רָם בְּאִיּוֹב
חָרָה אַפּוֹ עַל־צַדְּקוֹ נַפְשׁוֹ מֵאֱלֹהִים׃
3 וּבִשְׁלֹשֶׁת רֵעָיו חָרָה אַפּוֹ עַל אֲשֶׁר
לֹא־מָצְאוּ מַעֲנֶה וַיַּרְשִׁיעוּ אֶת־
4 אִיּוֹב׃ וֶאֱלִיהוּ חִכָּה אֶת־אִיּוֹב תיקון סופרים
בִּדְבָרִים כִּי זְקֵנִים־הֵמָּה מִמֶּנּוּ
5 לְיָמִים׃ וַיַּרְא אֱלִיהוּא כִּי אֵין מַעֲנֶה
בְּפִי שְׁלֹשֶׁת הָאֲנָשִׁים וַיִּחַר אַפּוֹ׃

32

These three men ceased replying to Job, for he considered
himself right. [2] Then Elihu son of Barachel the Buzite, of the
family of Ram, was angry—angry at Job because he thought himself right against God. [3] He was angry as well at his three friends,
because they could not reply, but merely condemned Job. [4] Elihu
waited out Job's speech, for they were all older than he. [5] But
when Elihu saw that the three men had nothing to reply, he was
angry.

6 וַיַּעַן ׀ אֱלִיהוּא בֶן־בַּרַכְאֵל הַבּוּזִי
וַיֹּאמַר
צָעִיר אֲנִי לְיָמִים וְאַתֶּם יְשִׁישִׁים
עַל־כֵּן זָחַלְתִּי וָאִירָא ׀
מֵחַוֺּת דֵּעִי אֶתְכֶם׃
7 אָמַרְתִּי יָמִים יְדַבֵּרוּ
וְרֹב שָׁנִים יֹדִיעוּ חָכְמָה׃
8 אָכֵן רוּחַ־הִיא בֶאֱנוֹשׁ
וְנִשְׁמַת שַׁדַּי תְּבִינֵם׃
9 לֹא־רַבִּים יֶחְכָּמוּ
וּזְקֵנִים יָבִינוּ מִשְׁפָּט׃
10 לָכֵן אָמַרְתִּי שִׁמְעָה־לִּי
אֲחַוֶּה דֵעִי אַף־אָנִי׃
11 הֵן הוֹחַלְתִּי ׀ לְדִבְרֵיכֶם
אָזִין עַד־תְּבוּנֹתֵיכֶם
עַד־תַּחְקְרוּן מִלִּין׃
12 וְעָדֵיכֶם אֶתְבּוֹנָן
וְהִנֵּה אֵין לְאִיּוֹב מוֹכִיחַ
עוֹנֶה אֲמָרָיו מִכֶּם׃
13 פֶּן־תֹּאמְרוּ מָצָאנוּ חָכְמָה
אֵל־יִדְּפֶנּוּ לֹא־אִישׁ׃
14 וְלֹא־עָרַךְ אֵלַי מִלִּין
וּבְאִמְרֵיכֶם לֹא אֲשִׁיבֶנּוּ׃

[6] Then Elihu son of Barachel the Buzite said in reply:

I have but few years, while you are old;
Therefore I was too awestruck and fearful
To hold forth among you.
[7] I thought, "Let age speak;
Let advanced years declare wise things."
[8] But truly it is the spirit in men,
The breath of Shaddai, that gives them understanding.
[9] It is not the aged who are wise,
The elders, who understand how to judge.
[10] Therefore I say, "Listen to me;
I also would hold forth."
[11] Here I have waited out your speeches,
I have given ear to your insights,
While you probed the issues;
[12] But as I attended to you,
I saw that none of you could argue with Job,
Or offer replies to his statements.
[13] I fear you will say, "We have found the wise course;
God will defeat him, not man."
[14] He did not set out his case against me,
Nor shall I use your reasons to reply to him.

חַ֣תּוּ לֹא־עָ֣נוּ ע֑וֹד 15

הֶעְתִּ֖יקוּ מֵהֶ֣ם מִלִּֽים׃

וְ֭הוֹחַלְתִּי כִּי־לֹ֣א יְדַבֵּ֑רוּ 16

כִּ֥י עָ֝מְד֗וּ לֹא־עָ֥נוּ עֽוֹד׃

אַעֲנֶ֣ה אַף־אֲנִ֣י חֶלְקִ֑י 17

אֲחַוֶּ֖ה דֵעִ֣י אַף־אָֽנִי׃

כִּ֣י מָלֵ֣תִי מִלִּ֑ים 18

הֱ֝צִיקַ֗תְנִי ר֣וּחַ בִּטְנִֽי׃

הִנֵּֽה־בִטְנִ֗י כְּיַ֥יִן לֹא־יִפָּתֵ֑חַ 19

כְּאֹב֥וֹת חֲ֝דָשִׁ֗ים יִבָּקֵֽעַ׃

אֲדַבְּרָ֥ה וְיִֽרְוַֽח־לִ֑י 20

אֶפְתַּ֖ח שְׂפָתַ֣י וְאֶעֱנֶֽה׃

אַל־נָ֭א אֶשָּׂ֣א פְנֵי־אִ֑ישׁ 21

וְאֶל־אָ֝דָ֗ם לֹ֣א אֲכַנֶּֽה׃

כִּ֤י לֹ֣א יָדַ֣עְתִּי אֲכַנֶּ֑ה 22

כִּ֝מְעַ֗ט יִשָּׂאֵ֥נִי עֹשֵֽׂנִי׃

לג

וְֽאוּלָ֗ם שְׁמַֽע־נָ֣א אִיּ֣וֹב מִלָּ֑י 1

וְֽכָל־דְּבָרַ֥י הַאֲזִֽינָה׃

הִנֵּה־נָ֭א פָּתַ֣חְתִּי פִ֑י 2

דִּבְּרָ֖ה לְשׁוֹנִ֣י בְחִכִּֽי׃

יֹֽשֶׁר־לִבִּ֥י אֲמָרָ֑י 3

וְדַ֥עַת שְׂ֝פָתַ֗י בָּר֥וּר מִלֵּֽלוּ׃

רֽוּחַ־אֵ֥ל עָשָׂ֑תְנִי 4

וְנִשְׁמַ֖ת שַׁדַּ֣י תְּחַיֵּֽנִי׃

אִם־תּוּכַ֥ל הֲשִׁיבֵ֑נִי 5

עֶרְכָ֥ה לְ֝פָנַ֗י הִתְיַצָּֽבָה׃

הֵן־אֲנִ֣י כְפִ֣יךָ לָאֵ֑ל 6

מֵ֝חֹ֗מֶר קֹרַ֥צְתִּי גַם־אָֽנִי׃

הִנֵּ֣ה אֵ֭מָתִי לֹ֣א תְבַעֲתֶ֑ךָּ 7

וְ֝אַכְפִּ֗י עָלֶ֥יךָ לֹא־יִכְבָּֽד׃

אַ֭ךְ אָמַ֣רְתָּ בְאָזְנָ֑י 8

וְק֖וֹל מִלִּ֣ין אֶשְׁמָֽע׃

זַ֥ךְ אֲנִ֗י בְּֽלִ֫י־פָ֥שַׁע 9

חַ֥ף אָנֹכִ֑י וְלֹ֖א עָוֺ֣ן לִֽי׃

הֵ֣ן תְּ֭נוּאוֹת עָלַ֣י יִמְצָ֑א 10

יַחְשְׁבֵ֖נִי לְאוֹיֵ֣ב לֽוֹ׃

יָשֵׂ֣ם בַּסַּ֣ד רַגְלָ֑י 11

יִ֝שְׁמֹ֗ר כָּל־אָרְחֹתָֽי׃

15 They have been broken and can no longer reply;
Words fail them.
16 I have waited till they stopped speaking,
Till they ended and no longer replied.
17 Now I also would have my say;
I too would like to hold forth,
18 For I am full of words;
The wind in my belly presses me.
19 My belly is like wine not yet opened,
Like jugs of new wine ready to burst.
20 Let me speak, then, and get relief;
Let me open my lips and reply.
21 I would not show regard for any man,
Or temper my speech for anyone's sake;
22 For I do not know how to temper my speech—
My Maker would soon carry me off!

33 But now, Job, listen to my words,
Give ear to all that I say.
2 Now I open my lips;
My tongue forms words in my mouth.
3 My words bespeak the uprightness of my heart;
My lips utter insight honestly.
4 The spirit of God formed me;
The breath of Shaddai sustains me.
5 If you can, answer me;
Argue against me, take your stand.
6 You and I are the same before God;
I too was nipped from clay.
7 You are not overwhelmed by fear of me;
My pressure does not weigh heavily on you.

8 Indeed, you have stated in my hearing,
I heard the words spoken,
9 "I am guiltless, free from transgression;
I am innocent, without iniquity.
10 But He finds reasons to oppose me,
Considers me His enemy.
11 He puts my feet in stocks,
Watches all my ways."

12 הֶן־זֹאת לֹא־צָדַקְתָּ אֶעֱנֶךָּ
כִּי־יִרְבֶּה אֱלוֹהַּ מֵאֱנוֹשׁ׃
13 מַדּוּעַ אֵלָיו רִיבוֹתָ
כִּי כָל־דְּבָרָיו לֹא יַעֲנֶה׃
14 כִּי־בְאַחַת יְדַבֶּר־אֵל
וּבִשְׁתַּיִם לֹא יְשׁוּרֶנָּה׃
15 בַּחֲלוֹם ׀ חֶזְיוֹן לַיְלָה
בִּנְפֹל תַּרְדֵּמָה עַל־אֲנָשִׁים
בִּתְנוּמוֹת עֲלֵי מִשְׁכָּב׃
16 אָז יִגְלֶה אֹזֶן אֲנָשִׁים
וּבְמֹסָרָם יַחְתֹּם׃
17 לְהָסִיר אָדָם מַעֲשֶׂה
וְגֵוָה מִגֶּבֶר יְכַסֶּה׃
18 יַחְשֹׂךְ נַפְשׁוֹ מִנִּי־שָׁחַת
וְחַיָּתוֹ מֵעֲבֹר בַּשָּׁלַח׃
19 וְהוּכַח בְּמַכְאוֹב עַל־מִשְׁכָּבוֹ
וְרִיב עֲצָמָיו אֵתָן׃ — ורוב ק׳
20 וְזִהֲמַתּוּ חַיָּתוֹ לָחֶם
וְנַפְשׁוֹ מַאֲכַל תַּאֲוָה׃
21 יִכֶל בְּשָׂרוֹ מֵרֹאִי
וְשֻׁפִּי עַצְמֹתָיו לֹא רֻאּוּ׃ — ושפו ק׳ — א׳ דגושה ובק״ס הרי״ש דגושה
22 וַתִּקְרַב לַשַּׁחַת נַפְשׁוֹ
וְחַיָּתוֹ לַמְמִתִים׃
23 אִם־יֵשׁ עָלָיו ׀ מַלְאָךְ
מֵלִיץ אֶחָד מִנִּי־אָלֶף
לְהַגִּיד לְאָדָם יָשְׁרוֹ׃
24 וַיְחֻנֶּנּוּ וַיֹּאמֶר
פְּדָעֵהוּ מֵרֶדֶת שָׁחַת
מָצָאתִי כֹפֶר׃
25 רֻטֲפַשׁ בְּשָׂרוֹ מִנֹּעַר
יָשׁוּב לִימֵי עֲלוּמָיו׃
26 יֶעְתַּר אֶל־אֱלוֹהַּ ׀ וַיִּרְצֵהוּ
וַיַּרְא פָּנָיו בִּתְרוּעָה
וַיָּשֶׁב לֶאֱנוֹשׁ צִדְקָתוֹ׃
27 יָשֹׁר ׀ עַל־אֲנָשִׁים וַיֹּאמֶר
חָטָאתִי וְיָשָׁר הֶעֱוֵיתִי
וְלֹא־שָׁוָה לִי׃
28 פָּדָה נַפְשִׁי מֵעֲבֹר בַּשָּׁחַת — נפשו ק׳
וְחַיָּתִי בָּאוֹר תִּרְאֶה׃ — וחיתו ק׳

12 In this you are not right;
I will answer you: God is greater than any man.
13 Why do you complain against Him
That He does not reply to any of man's charges?
14 For God speaks [a]time and again[a]
—Though man does not perceive it—
15 In a dream, a night vision,
When deep sleep falls on men,
While they slumber on their beds.
16 Then He opens men's understanding,
And by disciplining them leaves His signature
17 To turn man away from an action,
To suppress pride in man.
18 He spares him from the Pit,
His person, from perishing by the sword.
19 He is reproved by pains on his bed,
And the trembling in his bones is constant.
20 He detests food;
Fine food [is repulsive] to him.
21 His flesh wastes away till it cannot be seen,
And his bones are rubbed away till they are invisible.
22 He comes close to the Pit,
His life [verges] on death.
23 If he has a representative,
One advocate against a thousand
To declare the man's uprightness,
24 Then He has mercy on him and decrees,
"Redeem him from descending to the Pit,
For I have obtained his ransom;
25 Let his flesh be healthier[b] than in his youth;
Let him return to his younger days."
26 He prays to God and is accepted by Him;
He enters His presence with shouts of joy,
For He requites a man for his righteousness.
27 He[c] declares[b] to men,
"I have sinned; I have perverted what was right;
But I was not paid back for it."
28 He redeemed [d]him from passing into the Pit;
He[d] will enjoy the light.

[a-a] *Lit. "once . . . twice."*
[b] *Meaning of Heb. uncertain.*
[c] *I.e. the wicked*
[d-d] *Or, with* kethib, *"me . . . I."*

29 הֶן־כׇּל־אֵלֶּה יִפְעַל־אֵל
פַּעֲמַיִם שָׁלוֹשׁ עִם־גָּבֶר׃
30 לְהָשִׁיב נַפְשׁוֹ מִנִּי־שָׁחַת
לֵאוֹר בְּאוֹר הַחַיִּים׃

29 Truly, God does all these things
Two, three times to a man,
30 To bring him back from the Pit,
That he may bask in the light of life.

31 הַקְשֵׁב אִיּוֹב שְׁמַע־לִי
הַחֲרֵשׁ וְאָנֹכִי אֲדַבֵּר׃
32 אִם־יֵשׁ־מִלִּין הֲשִׁיבֵנִי
דַּבֵּר כִּי־חָפַצְתִּי צַדְּקֶךָּ׃
33 אִם־אַיִן אַתָּה שְׁמַע־לִי
הַחֲרֵשׁ וַאֲאַלֶּפְךָ חׇכְמָה׃

31 Pay heed, Job, and hear me;
Be still, and I will speak;
32 If you have what to say, answer me;
Speak, for I am eager to vindicate you.
33 But if not, you listen to me;
Be still, and I will teach you wisdom.

לד

34

1 וַיַּעַן אֱלִיהוּא וַיֹּאמַר׃

1 Elihu said in reply:

2 שִׁמְעוּ חֲכָמִים מִלָּי
וְיֹדְעִים הַאֲזִינוּ לִי׃
3 כִּי־אֹזֶן מִלִּין תִּבְחָן
וְחֵךְ יִטְעַם לֶאֱכֹל׃
4 מִשְׁפָּט נִבְחֲרָה־לָּנוּ
נֵדְעָה בֵינֵינוּ מַה־טּוֹב׃
5 כִּי־אָמַר אִיּוֹב צָדַקְתִּי פתח באתנח
וְאֵל הֵסִיר מִשְׁפָּטִי׃
6 עַל־מִשְׁפָּטִי אֲכַזֵּב
אָנוּשׁ חִצִּי בְלִי־פָשַׁע׃

2 Listen, O wise men, to my words;
You learned, give ear to me.
3 For the ear tests arguments
As the palate tastes food.
4 Let us decide for ourselves what is just;
Let us know among ourselves what is good.
5 For Job has said, "I am right;
God has deprived me of justice.
6 I declare the judgment against me false;
My arrow-wound is deadly, though I am free from transgression."

7 מִי־גֶבֶר כְּאִיּוֹב
יִשְׁתֶּה־לַּעַג כַּמָּיִם׃
8 וְאָרַח לְחֶבְרָה עִם־פֹּעֲלֵי אָוֶן
וְלָלֶכֶת עִם־אַנְשֵׁי־רֶשַׁע׃
9 כִּי־אָמַר לֹא יִסְכׇּן־גָּבֶר
בִּרְצֹתוֹ עִם־אֱלֹהִים׃

7 What man is like Job,
Who drinks mockery like water;
8 Who makes common cause with evildoers,
And goes with wicked men?
9 For he says, "Man gains nothing
When he is in God's favor."

10 לָכֵן ׀ אַנְשֵׁי לֵבָב שִׁמְעוּ לִי
חָלִלָה לָאֵל מֵרֶשַׁע
וְשַׁדַּי מֵעָוֶל׃
11 כִּי פֹעַל אָדָם יְשַׁלֶּם־לוֹ
וּכְאֹרַח אִישׁ יַמְצִאֶנּוּ׃
12 אַף־אׇמְנָם אֵל לֹא־יַרְשִׁיעַ
וְשַׁדַּי לֹא־יְעַוֵּת מִשְׁפָּט׃
13 מִי־פָקַד עָלָיו אָרְצָה
וּמִי שָׂם תֵּבֵל כֻּלָּהּ׃

10 Therefore, men of understanding, listen to me;
Wickedness be far from God,
Wrongdoing, from Shaddai!
11 For He pays a man according to his actions,
And provides for him according to his conduct;
12 For God surely does not act wickedly;
Shaddai does not pervert justice.
13 Who placed the earth in His charge?
Who ordered the entire world?

14 אִם־יָשִׂים אֵלָיו לִבּוֹ לְמדנחאי ישיב כתיב ישים ק׳
רוּחוֹ וְנִשְׁמָתוֹ אֵלָיו יֶאֱסֹף׃
15 יִגְוַע כָּל־בָּשָׂר יָחַד
וְאָדָם עַל־עָפָר יָשׁוּב׃

16 וְאִם־בִּינָה שִׁמְעָה־זֹּאת
הַאֲזִינָה לְקוֹל מִלָּי׃
17 הַאַף שׂוֹנֵא מִשְׁפָּט יַחֲבוֹשׁ
וְאִם־צַדִּיק כַּבִּיר תַּרְשִׁיעַ׃
18 הַאֲמֹר לְמֶלֶךְ בְּלִיָּעַל
רָשָׁע אֶל־נְדִיבִים׃
19 אֲשֶׁר לֹא־נָשָׂא ׀ פְּנֵי שָׂרִים
וְלֹא נִכַּר־שׁוֹעַ לִפְנֵי־דָל
כִּי־מַעֲשֵׂה יָדָיו כֻּלָּם׃
20 רֶגַע ׀ יָמֻתוּ וַחֲצוֹת לָיְלָה
יְגֹעֲשׁוּ עָם וְיַעֲבֹרוּ
וְיָסִירוּ אַבִּיר לֹא בְיָד׃
21 כִּי־עֵינָיו עַל־דַּרְכֵי־אִישׁ
וְכָל־צְעָדָיו יִרְאֶה׃
22 אֵין־חֹשֶׁךְ וְאֵין צַלְמָוֶת
לְהִסָּתֶר שָׁם פֹּעֲלֵי אָוֶן׃
23 כִּי לֹא עַל־אִישׁ יָשִׂים עוֹד
לַהֲלֹךְ אֶל־אֵל בַּמִּשְׁפָּט׃
24 יָרֹעַ כַּבִּירִים לֹא־חֵקֶר
וַיַּעֲמֵד אֲחֵרִים תַּחְתָּם׃
25 לָכֵן יַכִּיר מַעְבָּדֵיהֶם
וְהָפַךְ לַיְלָה וְיִדַּכָּאוּ׃
26 תַּחַת־רְשָׁעִים סְפָקָם
בִּמְקוֹם רֹאִים׃
27 אֲשֶׁר עַל־כֵּן סָרוּ מֵאַחֲרָיו
וְכָל־דְּרָכָיו לֹא הִשְׂכִּילוּ׃
28 לְהָבִיא עָלָיו צַעֲקַת־דָּל
וְצַעֲקַת עֲנִיִּים יִשְׁמָע׃
29 וְהוּא יַשְׁקִט ׀ וּמִי יַרְשִׁעַ
וְיַסְתֵּר פָּנִים וּמִי יְשׁוּרֶנּוּ
וְעַל־גּוֹי וְעַל־אָדָם יָחַד׃
30 מִמְּלֹךְ אָדָם חָנֵף
מִמֹּקְשֵׁי עָם׃
31 כִּי אֶל־אֵל הֶאָמַר נָשָׂאתִי
לֹא אֶחְבֹּל׃
32 בִּלְעֲדֵי אֶחֱזֶה אַתָּה הֹרֵנִי
אִם־עָוֶל פָּעַלְתִּי לֹא אֹסִיף׃

14 If He but intends it,
He can call back His spirit and breath;
15 All flesh would at once expire,
And mankind return to dust.

16 If you would understand, listen to this;
Give ear to what I say.
17 Would one who hates justice govern?
Would you condemn the Just Mighty One?
18 Would you call a king a scoundrel,
Great men, wicked?
19 He is not partial to princes;
The noble are not preferred to the wretched;
For all of them are the work of His hands.
20 Some die suddenly in the middle of the night;
People are in turmoil and pass on;
Even great men are removed—not by human hands.
21 For His eyes are upon a man's ways;
He observes his every step.
22 Neither darkness nor gloom offer
A hiding-place for evildoers.
23 He has no set time for man
To appear before God in judgment.
24 He shatters mighty men without number
And sets others in their place.
25 Truly, He knows their deeds;
Night is over, and they are crushed.
26 He strikes them down with the wicked
Where people can see,
27 Because they have been disloyal to Him
And not understood any of His ways;
28 Thus He lets the cry of the poor come before Him;
He listens to the cry of the needy.
29 When He is silent, who will condemn?
If He hides His face, who will see Him,
Be it nation or man?
30 The impious men rule no more,
Nor do those who ensnare the people.
31 Has he said to God,
"I will bear [my punishment] and offend no more.
32 What I cannot see You teach me.
If I have done iniquity, I shall not do so again"?

33 הַמֵעִמְּךָ֨ יְשַׁלְמֶ֥נָּה | כִּֽי־מָאַ֗סְתָּ
כִּֽי־אַתָּ֣ה תִבְחַ֣ר וְלֹא־אָ֑נִי
וּמַה־יָדַ֥עְתָּ דַבֵּֽר:

34 אַנְשֵׁ֣י לֵ֭בָב יֹ֣אמְרוּ לִ֑י
וְגֶ֥בֶר חָ֝כָ֗ם שֹׁמֵ֥עַֽ לִֽי:

35 אִ֭יּוֹב לֹא־בְדַ֣עַת יְדַבֵּ֑ר
וּ֝דְבָרָ֗יו לֹ֣א בְהַשְׂכֵּֽיל:

36 אָבִ֗י יִבָּחֵ֣ן אִיּ֣וֹב עַד־נֶ֑צַח
עַל־תְּ֝שֻׁבֹ֗ת בְּאַנְשֵׁי־אָֽוֶן:

37 כִּ֤י יֹסִ֣יף עַל־חַטָּאת֣וֹ פֶ֑שַׁע
בֵּינֵ֣ינוּ יִסְפּ֑וֹק
וְיֶ֖רֶב אֲמָרָ֣יו לָאֵֽל:

לה

1 וַיַּ֖עַן אֱלִיה֣וּ וַיֹּאמַֽר: בנ״א אליהוא

2 הֲ֭זֹאת חָשַׁ֣בְתָּ לְמִשְׁפָּ֑ט
אָ֝מַ֗רְתָּ צִדְקִ֥י מֵאֵֽל:

3 כִּֽי־תֹ֖אמַר מַה־יִּסְכָּן־לָ֑ךְ
מָֽה־אֹ֝עִ֗יל מֵֽחַטָּאתִֽי:

4 אֲ֭נִי אֲשִֽׁיבְךָ֣ מִלִּ֑ין
וְאֶת־רֵעֶ֥יךָ עִמָּֽךְ:

5 הַבֵּ֣ט שָׁמַ֣יִם וּרְאֵ֑ה
וְשׁ֥וּר שְׁ֝חָקִ֗ים גָּבְה֥וּ מִמֶּֽךָּ:

6 אִם־חָ֭טָאתָ מַה־תִּפְעָל־בּ֑וֹ
וְרַבּ֥וּ פְ֝שָׁעֶ֗יךָ מַה־תַּעֲשֶׂה־לּֽוֹ:

7 אִם־צָ֭דַקְתָּ מַה־תִּתֶּן־ל֑וֹ
א֥וֹ מַה־מִּיָּדְךָ֥ יִקָּֽח:

8 לְאִישׁ־כָּמ֥וֹךָ רִשְׁעֶ֑ךָ
וּלְבֶן־אָ֝דָ֗ם צִדְקָתֶֽךָ:

9 מֵ֭רֹב עֲשׁוּקִ֣ים יַזְעִ֑יקוּ
יְשַׁוְּע֖וּ מִזְּר֣וֹעַ רַבִּֽים:

10 וְֽלֹא־אָמַ֗ר אַ֭יֵּה אֱל֣וֹהַּ עֹשָׂ֑י
נֹתֵ֖ן זְמִר֣וֹת בַּלָּֽיְלָה:

11 מַ֭לְּפֵנוּ מִבַּהֲמ֣וֹת אָ֑רֶץ
וּמֵע֖וֹף הַשָּׁמַ֣יִם יְחַכְּמֵֽנוּ:

12 שָׁ֣ם יִ֭צְעֲקוּ וְלֹ֣א יַעֲנֶ֑ה

33 Should He requite as you see fit?
But you have despised [Him]!
You must decide, not I;
Speak what you know.
34 Men of understanding say to me,
Wise men who hear me,
35 "Job does not speak with knowledge;
His words lack understanding."
36 Would that Job were tried to the limit
For answers which befit sinful men.
37 He adds to his sin;
He increases his transgression among us;
He multiplies his statements against God.

35 Elihu said in reply:

2 Do you think it just
To say, "I am right against God"?
3 If you ask how it benefits you,
"What have I gained from not sinning?"
4 I shall give you a reply,
You, along with your friends.
5 Behold the heavens and see;
Look at the skies high above you.
6 If you sin, what do you do to Him?
If your transgressions are many,
How do you affect Him?
7 If you are righteous,
What do you give Him;
What does He receive from your hand?
8 Your wickedness affects men like yourself;
Your righteousness, mortals.

9 Because of contention the oppressed cry out;
They shout because of the power of the great.
10 But none says, "Where is my God, my Maker,
Who gives strength in the night;
11 Who gives us more knowledge than the beasts of the
    earth,
Makes us wiser than the birds of the sky?"
12 Then they cry out, but He does not respond

מִפְּנֵי גְּאוֹן רָעִים׃
13 אַךְ־שָׁוְא לֹא־יִשְׁמַע ׀ אֵל
וְשַׁדַּי לֹא יְשׁוּרֶנָּה׃
14 אַף כִּי־תֹאמַר לֹא תְשׁוּרֶנּוּ
דִּין לְפָנָיו וּתְחוֹלֵל לוֹ׃

Because of the arrogance of evil men.
13 Surely it is false that God does not listen,
That Shaddai does not take note of it.
14 Though you say, "You do not take note of it,"
The case is before Him;
So wait for Him.

15 וְעַתָּה כִּי־אַיִן פָּקַד אַפּוֹ
וְלֹא־יָדַע בַּפַּשׁ מְאֹד׃

15 [a]-But since now it does not seem so,
He vents his anger;
He does not realize that it may be long drawn out.-[a]

16 וְאִיּוֹב הֶבֶל יִפְצֶה־פִּיהוּ
בִּבְלִי־דַעַת מִלִּין יַכְבִּר׃

16 Hence Job mouths empty words,
And piles up words without knowledge.

לו
1 וַיֹּסֶף אֱלִיהוּא וַיֹּאמַר׃

36

1 Then Elihu spoke once more.

2 כַּתַּר־לִי זְעֵיר וַאֲחַוֶּךָּ
כִּי־עוֹד לֶאֱלוֹהַּ מִלִּים׃
3 אֶשָּׂא דֵעִי לְמֵרָחוֹק
וּלְפֹעֲלִי אֶתֵּן־צֶדֶק׃
4 כִּי־אָמְנָם לֹא־שֶׁקֶר מִלָּי
תְּמִים דֵּעוֹת עִמָּךְ׃

2 Wait a little and let me hold forth;
There is still more to say for God.
3 I will make my opinions widely known;
I will justify my Maker.
4 In truth, my words are not false;
A man of sound opinions is before you.

5 הֶן־אֵל כַּבִּיר וְלֹא יִמְאָס
כַּבִּיר כֹּחַ לֵב׃
6 לֹא־יְחַיֶּה רָשָׁע
וּמִשְׁפַּט עֲנִיִּים יִתֵּן׃
7 לֹא־יִגְרַע מִצַּדִּיק עֵינָיו
וְאֶת־מְלָכִים לַכִּסֵּא
וַיֹּשִׁיבֵם לָנֶצַח וַיִּגְבָּהוּ׃
8 וְאִם־אֲסוּרִים בַּזִּקִּים
יִלָּכְדוּן בְּחַבְלֵי־עֹנִי׃
9 וַיַּגֵּד לָהֶם פָּעֳלָם
וּפִשְׁעֵיהֶם כִּי יִתְגַּבָּרוּ׃
10 וַיִּגֶל אָזְנָם לַמּוּסָר
וַיֹּאמֶר כִּי־יְשׁוּבוּן מֵאָוֶן׃
11 אִם־יִשְׁמְעוּ וְיַעֲבֹדוּ
יְכַלּוּ יְמֵיהֶם בַּטּוֹב
וּשְׁנֵיהֶם בַּנְּעִימִים׃
12 וְאִם־לֹא יִשְׁמְעוּ בְּשֶׁלַח יַעֲבֹרוּ
וְיִגְוְעוּ בִּבְלִי דָעַת׃

5 See, God is mighty; He is not contemptuous;
He is mighty in strength and mind.
6 He does not let the wicked live;
He grants justice to the lowly.
7 He does not withdraw His eyes from the righteous;
With kings on thrones
He seats them forever, and they are exalted.
8 If they are bound in shackles
And caught in trammels of affliction,
9 He is declaring to them what they have done,
And that their transgressions are excessive;
10 He is opening their understanding by discipline,
And ordering them back from mischief.
11 If they will serve obediently,
They shall spend their days in happiness,
Their years in delight.
12 But if they are not obedient,
They shall perish by the sword,
Die for lack of understanding.

[a-a] *Meaning of Heb. uncertain.*

13 וְֽחַנְפֵי־לֵב יָשִׂימוּ אָף
לֹא יְשַׁוְּעוּ כִּי אֲסָרָם׃
14 תָּמֹת בַּנֹּעַר נַפְשָׁם
וְחַיָּתָם בַּקְּדֵשִׁים׃
15 יְחַלֵּץ עָנִי בְעָנְיוֹ
וְיִגֶל בַּלַּחַץ אָזְנָם׃
16 וְאַף הֲסִיתְךָ ׀ מִפִּי־צָר
רַחַב לֹא־מוּצָק תַּחְתֶּיהָ
וְנַחַת שֻׁלְחָנְךָ מָלֵא דָשֶׁן׃
17 וְדִין־רָשָׁע מָלֵאתָ
דִּין וּמִשְׁפָּט יִתְמֹכוּ׃
18 כִּי־חֵמָה פֶּן־יְסִיתְךָ בְסָפֶק
וְרָב־כֹּפֶר אַל־יַטֶּךָּ׃
19 הֲיַעֲרֹךְ שׁוּעֲךָ לֹא בְצָר
וְכֹל מַאֲמַצֵּי־כֹחַ׃
20 אַל־תִּשְׁאַף הַלָּיְלָה
לַעֲלוֹת עַמִּים תַּחְתָּם׃
21 הִשָּׁמֶר אַל־תֵּפֶן אֶל־אָוֶן
כִּי עַל־זֶה בָּחַרְתָּ מֵעֹנִי׃
22 הֶן־אֵל יַשְׂגִּיב בְּכֹחוֹ
מִי כָמֹהוּ מוֹרֶה׃
23 מִי־פָקַד עָלָיו דַּרְכּוֹ
וּמִי־אָמַר פָּעַלְתָּ עַוְלָה׃
24 זְכֹר כִּי־תַשְׂגִּיא פָעֳלוֹ
אֲשֶׁר שֹׁרְרוּ אֲנָשִׁים׃
25 כָּל־אָדָם חָזוּ־בוֹ
אֱנוֹשׁ יַבִּיט מֵרָחוֹק׃
26 הֶן־אֵל שַׂגִּיא וְלֹא נֵדָע
מִסְפַּר שָׁנָיו וְלֹא־חֵקֶר׃
27 כִּי יְגָרַע נִטְפֵי־מָיִם
יָזֹקּוּ מָטָר לְאֵדוֹ׃
28 אֲשֶׁר־יִזְּלוּ שְׁחָקִים
יִרְעֲפוּ עֲלֵי ׀ אָדָם רָב׃
29 אַף אִם־יָבִין מִפְרְשֵׂי־עָב
תְּשֻׁאוֹת סֻכָּתוֹ׃
30 הֵן־פָּרַשׂ עָלָיו אוֹרוֹ
וְשָׁרְשֵׁי הַיָּם כִּסָּה׃
31 כִּי־בָם יָדִין עַמִּים
יִתֶּן־אֹכֶל לְמַכְבִּיר׃
32 עַל־כַּפַּיִם כִּסָּה־אוֹר
וַיְצַו עָלֶיהָ בְמַפְגִּיעַ׃

13 But the impious in heart become enraged;
They do not cry for help when He afflicts them.
14 They die in their youth;
[Expire] among the depraved.
15 He rescues the lowly from their affliction,
And opens their understanding through distress.
16 Indeed, He draws you away from the brink of distress
To a broad place where there is no constraint;
Your table is laid out with rich food.
17 Though you are obsessed with the case of the wicked,
The justice of the case will be upheld.
18 Let anger at his affluence not mislead you;
Let much bribery not turn you aside.
19 [a]Will your limitless wealth avail you,[a]
All your powerful efforts?
20 Do not long for the night
When peoples vanish where they are.
21 Beware! Do not turn to mischief,
Because of which you have been tried by affliction.
22 See, God is beyond reach in His power;
Who governs like Him?
23 Who ever reproached Him for His conduct?
Who ever said, "You have done wrong"?
24 Remember, then, to magnify His work,
Of which men have sung,
25 Which all men have beheld,
Men have seen, from a distance.
26 See, God is greater than we can know;
The number of His years cannot be counted.
27 He forms the droplets of water,
Which cluster into rain, from His mist.
28 The skies rain;
They pour down on all mankind.
29 Can one, indeed, contemplate the expanse of clouds,
The thunderings from His pavilion?
30 See, He spreads His lightning over it;
It fills the bed of the sea.
31 By these things He controls peoples;
He gives food in abundance.
32 Lightning fills His hands;
He orders it to hit the mark.

a-a *Meaning of Heb. uncertain.*

33 יַגִּיד עָלָיו רֵעוֹ
מִקְנֶה אַף עַל־עוֹלֶה׃

לז

1 אַף־לְזֹאת יֶחֱרַד לִבִּי
וְיִתַּר מִמְּקוֹמוֹ׃
2 שִׁמְעוּ שָׁמוֹעַ בְּרֹגֶז קֹלוֹ
וְהֶגֶה מִפִּיו יֵצֵא׃
3 תַּחַת־כָּל־הַשָּׁמַיִם יִשְׁרֵהוּ
וְאוֹרוֹ עַל־כַּנְפוֹת הָאָרֶץ׃
4 אַחֲרָיו ׀ יִשְׁאַג־קוֹל
יַרְעֵם בְּקוֹל גְּאוֹנוֹ
וְלֹא יְעַקְּבֵם כִּי־יִשָּׁמַע קוֹלוֹ׃
5 יַרְעֵם אֵל בְּקוֹלוֹ נִפְלָאוֹת
עֹשֶׂה גְדֹלוֹת וְלֹא נֵדָע׃
6 כִּי לַשֶּׁלַג ׀ יֹאמַר הֱוֵא־אָרֶץ
וְגֶשֶׁם מָטָר וְגֶשֶׁם מִטְרוֹת עֻזּוֹ׃
7 בְּיַד־כָּל־אָדָם יַחְתּוֹם
לָדַעַת כָּל־אַנְשֵׁי מַעֲשֵׂהוּ׃
8 וַתָּבֹא חַיָּה בְמוֹ־אָרֶב
וּבִמְעוֹנֹתֶיהָ תִשְׁכֹּן׃
9 מִן־הַחֶדֶר תָּבוֹא סוּפָה
וּמִמְּזָרִים קָרָה׃
10 מִנִּשְׁמַת־אֵל יִתֶּן־קָרַח
וְרֹחַב מַיִם בְּמוּצָק׃
11 אַף־בְּרִי יַטְרִיחַ עָב
יָפִיץ עֲנַן אוֹרוֹ׃
12 וְהוּא מְסִבּוֹת ׀ מִתְהַפֵּךְ בְּתַחְבּוּלֹתָו בתחבולתיו ק׳
לְפָעֳלָם כֹּל אֲשֶׁר יְצַוֵּם ׀
עַל־פְּנֵי תֵבֵל אָרְצָה׃
13 אִם־לְשֵׁבֶט אִם־לְאַרְצוֹ
אִם־לְחֶסֶד יַמְצִאֵהוּ׃

14 הַאֲזִינָה זֹּאת אִיּוֹב
עֲמֹד וְהִתְבּוֹנֵן ׀ נִפְלְאוֹת אֵל׃
15 הֲתֵדַע בְּשׂוּם־אֱלוֹהַּ עֲלֵיהֶם
וְהוֹפִיעַ אוֹר עֲנָנוֹ׃
16 הֲתֵדַע עַל־מִפְלְשֵׂי־עָב
מִפְלְאוֹת תְּמִים דֵּעִים׃

17 אֲשֶׁר־בְּגָדֶיךָ חַמִּים

33 Its noise tells of Him.
[a]The kindling of anger against iniquity.[a]

37

Because of this, too, my heart quakes,
And leaps from its place.
2 Just listen to the noise of His rumbling,
To the sound that comes out of His mouth.
3 He lets it loose beneath the entire heavens—
His lightning to the ends of the earth.
4 After it, He lets out a roar;
He thunders in His majestic voice.
No one can find a trace of it by the time His voice is heard.
5 God thunders marvelously with His voice;
He works wonders that we cannot understand.
6 He commands the snow, "Fall to the ground!"
And the downpour of rain, His mighty downpour of rain,
7 Is as a sign on every man's hand,
That all men may know His doings.
8 Then the beast enters its lair,
And remains in its den.
9 The storm wind comes from its chamber,
And the cold from the constellations.
10 By the breath of God ice is formed,
And the expanse of water becomes solid.
11 He also loads the clouds with moisture
And scatters His lightning-clouds.
12 [a]He keeps turning events by His stratagems,[a]
That they might accomplish all that He commands them
Throughout the inhabited earth,
13 Causing each of them to happen to His land,
Whether as a scourge or as a blessing.

14 Give ear to this, Job;
Stop to consider the marvels of God.
15 Do you know what charge God lays upon them
When His lightning-clouds shine?
16 Do you know the marvels worked upon the expanse of clouds
By Him whose understanding is perfect,
17 [a]How your clothes become warm[a]

[a-a] *Meaning of Heb. uncertain.*

בְּהַשְׁקִט אֶרֶץ מִדָּרוֹם׃
18 תַּרְקִיעַ עִמּוֹ לִשְׁחָקִים
חֲזָקִים כִּרְאִי מוּצָק׃
19 הוֹדִיעֵנוּ מַה־נֹּאמַר לוֹ
לֹא נַעֲרֹךְ מִפְּנֵי־חֹשֶׁךְ׃
20 הַיְסֻפַּר־לוֹ כִּי אֲדַבֵּר
אִם־אָמַר אִישׁ כִּי יְבֻלָּע׃
21 וְעַתָּה ׀ לֹא־רָאוּ אוֹר
בָּהִיר הוּא בַּשְּׁחָקִים
וְרוּחַ עָבְרָה וַתְּטַהֲרֵם׃
22 מִצָּפוֹן זָהָב יֶאֱתֶה
עַל־אֱלוֹהַּ נוֹרָא הוֹד׃
23 שַׁדַּי לֹא־מְצָאנֻהוּ שַׂגִּיא־כֹחַ
וּמִשְׁפָּט וְרֹב־צְדָקָה לֹא יְעַנֶּה׃

24 לָכֵן יְרֵאוּהוּ אֲנָשִׁים
לֹא יִרְאֶה כָּל־חַכְמֵי־לֵב׃

When the land is becalmed by the south wind?
18 Can you soar like Him to heaven,
Firm as a mirror of cast metal?
19 Inform us, then, what we may say to Him;
We cannot argue because [we are in] darkness.
20 Is anything conveyed to Him when I speak?
Can a man say anything when he is confused?
21 Now, then, one cannot see the sun,
Though it be bright in the heavens,
Until the wind comes and clears them [of clouds].
22 By the north wind the golden rays emerge;
The splendor about God is awesome.
23 Shaddai—we cannot attain to Him;
He is great in power and justice
And abundant in righteousness; He does not torment.
24 Therefore, men are in awe of Him
Whom none of the wise can perceive.

לח
1 וַיַּעַן־יְהוָה אֶת־אִיּוֹב
מִנ ׀ הַסְּעָרָה וַיֹּאמַר׃ מן ק׳
2 מִי זֶה ׀ מַחְשִׁיךְ עֵצָה
בְמִלִּין בְּלִי־דָעַת׃
3 אֱזָר־נָא כְגֶבֶר חֲלָצֶיךָ
וְאֶשְׁאָלְךָ וְהוֹדִיעֵנִי׃

4 אֵיפֹה הָיִיתָ בְּיָסְדִי־אָרֶץ
הַגֵּד אִם־יָדַעְתָּ בִינָה׃
5 מִי־שָׂם מְמַדֶּיהָ כִּי תֵדָע
אוֹ מִי־נָטָה עָלֶיהָ קָּו׃
6 עַל־מָה אֲדָנֶיהָ הָטְבָּעוּ
אוֹ מִי־יָרָה אֶבֶן פִּנָּתָהּ׃
7 בְּרָן־יַחַד כּוֹכְבֵי בֹקֶר
וַיָּרִיעוּ כָּל־בְּנֵי אֱלֹהִים׃

8 וַיָּסֶךְ בִּדְלָתַיִם יָם
בְּגִיחוֹ מֵרֶחֶם יֵצֵא׃
9 בְּשׂוּמִי עָנָן לְבֻשׁוֹ
וַעֲרָפֶל חֲתֻלָּתוֹ׃
10 וָאֶשְׁבֹּר עָלָיו חֻקִּי
וָאָשִׂים בְּרִיחַ וּדְלָתָיִם׃

38

Then the LORD replied to Job out of the tempest and said:

2 Who is this who darkens counsel,
Speaking without knowledge?
3 Gird your loins like a man;
I will ask and you will inform Me.

4 Where were you when I laid the earth's foundations?
Speak if you have understanding.
5 Do you know who fixed its dimensions
Or who measured it with a line?
6 Onto what were its bases sunk?
Who set its cornerstone
7 When the morning stars sang together,
And all the divine beings shouted for joy?

8 Who closed the sea behind doors
When it gushed forth out of the womb,
9 When I clothed it in clouds,
Swaddled it in dense clouds,
10 When I made breakers My limit for it,
And set up its bar and doors,

11 וָאֹמַר עַד־פֹּה תָבוֹא וְלֹא תֹסִיף
וּפֹא יָשִׁית בִּגְאוֹן גַּלֶּיךָ׃ א׳ במקום ה׳

[11] And said, "You may come so far and no farther;
Here your surging waves will stop"?

12 הְמִיָּמֶיךָ צִוִּיתָ בֹּקֶר
יִדַּעְתָּה שַׁחַר מְקֹמוֹ׃ ידעת השחר ק׳
13 לֶאֱחֹז בְּכַנְפוֹת הָאָרֶץ
וְיִנָּעֲרוּ רְשָׁעִים מִמֶּנָּה׃ ע׳ תלויה
14 תִּתְהַפֵּךְ כְּחֹמֶר חוֹתָם
וְיִתְיַצְּבוּ כְּמוֹ לְבוּשׁ׃
15 וְיִמָּנַע מֵרְשָׁעִים אוֹרָם ע׳ תלויה
וּזְרוֹעַ רָמָה תִּשָּׁבֵר׃

[12] Have you ever commanded the day to break,
Assigned the dawn its place,
[13] So that it seizes the corners of the earth
And shakes the wicked out of it?
[14] It changes like clay under the seal
Till [its hues] are fixed like those of a garment.
[15] Their light is withheld from the wicked,
And the upraised arm is broken.

16 הֲבָאתָ עַד־נִבְכֵי־יָם
וּבְחֵקֶר תְּהוֹם הִתְהַלָּכְתָּ׃
17 הֲנִגְלוּ לְךָ שַׁעֲרֵי־מָוֶת
וְשַׁעֲרֵי צַלְמָוֶת תִּרְאֶה׃
18 הִתְבֹּנַנְתָּ עַד־רַחֲבֵי־אָרֶץ
הַגֵּד אִם־יָדַעְתָּ כֻלָּהּ׃

[16] Have you penetrated to the sources of the sea,
Or walked in the recesses of the deep?
[17] Have the gates of death been disclosed to you?
Have you seen the gates of deep darkness?
[18] Have you surveyed the expanses of the earth?
If you know of these—tell Me.

19 אֵי־זֶה הַדֶּרֶךְ יִשְׁכָּן־אוֹר
וְחֹשֶׁךְ אֵי־זֶה מְקֹמוֹ׃
20 כִּי תִקָּחֶנּוּ אֶל־גְּבוּלוֹ
וְכִי תָבִין נְתִיבוֹת בֵּיתוֹ׃
21 יָדַעְתָּ כִּי־אָז תִּוָּלֵד
וּמִסְפַּר יָמֶיךָ רַבִּים׃

[19] Which path leads to where light dwells,
And where is the place of darkness,
[20] That you may take it to its domain
And know the way to its home?
[21] Surely you know, for you were born then,
And the number of your years is many!

22 הֲבָאתָ אֶל־אֹצְרוֹת שָׁלֶג
וְאוֹצְרוֹת בָּרָד תִּרְאֶה׃
23 אֲשֶׁר חָשַׂכְתִּי לְעֶת צָר
לְיוֹם קְרָב וּמִלְחָמָה׃
24 אֵי־זֶה הַדֶּרֶךְ יֵחָלֶק אוֹר
יָפֵץ קָדִים עֲלֵי־אָרֶץ׃
25 מִי־פִלַּג לַשֶּׁטֶף תְּעָלָה
וְדֶרֶךְ לַחֲזִיז קֹלוֹת׃
26 לְהַמְטִיר עַל־אֶרֶץ לֹא־אִישׁ
מִדְבָּר לֹא־אָדָם בּוֹ׃
27 לְהַשְׂבִּיעַ שֹׁאָה וּמְשֹׁאָה
וּלְהַצְמִיחַ מֹצָא דֶשֶׁא׃
28 הֲיֵשׁ לַמָּטָר אָב
אוֹ מִי־הוֹלִיד אֶגְלֵי־טָל׃
29 מִבֶּטֶן מִי יָצָא הַקָּרַח

[22] Have you penetrated the vaults of snow,
Seen the vaults of hail,
[23] Which I have put aside for a time of adversity,
For a day of war and battle?
[24] By what path is the west wind[a] dispersed,
The east wind scattered over the earth?
[25] Who cut a channel for the torrents
And a path for the thunderstorms,
[26] To rain down on the uninhabited land,
On the wilderness where no man is,
[27] To saturate the desolate wasteland,
And make the crop of grass sprout forth?
[28] Does the rain have a father?
Who begot the dewdrops?
[29] From whose belly came forth the ice?

[a] *As Aramaic* 'urya.

וּכְפֹר שָׁמַיִם מִי יְלָדוֹ׃
30 כָּאֶבֶן מַיִם יִתְחַבָּאוּ
וּפְנֵי תְהוֹם יִתְלַכָּדוּ׃

31 הַתְקַשֵּׁר מַעֲדַנּוֹת כִּימָה
אוֹ־מוֹשְׁכוֹת כְּסִיל תְּפַתֵּחַ׃
32 הֲתֹצִיא מַזָּרוֹת בְּעִתּוֹ
וְעַיִשׁ עַל־בָּנֶיהָ תַנְחֵם׃
33 הֲיָדַעְתָּ חֻקּוֹת שָׁמָיִם
אִם־תָּשִׂים מִשְׁטָרוֹ בָאָרֶץ׃

34 הֲתָרִים לָעָב קוֹלֶךָ
וְשִׁפְעַת־מַיִם תְּכַסֶּךָּ׃
35 הַתְשַׁלַּח בְּרָקִים וְיֵלֵכוּ
וְיֹאמְרוּ לְךָ הִנֵּנוּ׃
36 מִי־שָׁת בַּטֻּחוֹת חָכְמָה
אוֹ מִי־נָתַן לַשֶּׂכְוִי בִינָה׃
37 מִי־יְסַפֵּר שְׁחָקִים בְּחָכְמָה
וְנִבְלֵי שָׁמַיִם מִי יַשְׁכִּיב׃
38 בְּצֶקֶת עָפָר לַמּוּצָק
וּרְגָבִים יְדֻבָּקוּ׃

39 הֲתָצוּד לְלָבִיא טָרֶף
וְחַיַּת כְּפִירִים תְּמַלֵּא׃
40 כִּי־יָשֹׁחוּ בַמְּעוֹנוֹת
יֵשְׁבוּ בַסֻּכָּה לְמוֹ־אָרֶב׃
41 מִי יָכִין לָעֹרֵב צֵידוֹ
כִּי־יְלָדָו אֶל־אֵל יְשַׁוֵּעוּ ילדיו ק׳
יִתְעוּ לִבְלִי־אֹכֶל׃

לט
1 הֲיָדַעְתָּ עֵת לֶדֶת יַעֲלֵי־סָלַע
חֹלֵל אַיָּלוֹת תִּשְׁמֹר׃

2 תִּסְפֹּר יְרָחִים תְּמַלֶּאנָה
וְיָדַעְתָּ עֵת לִדְתָּנָה׃
3 תִּכְרַעְנָה יַלְדֵיהֶן תְּפַלַּחְנָה
חֶבְלֵיהֶם תְּשַׁלַּחְנָה׃ פתח באתנח וס״פ
4 יַחְלְמוּ בְנֵיהֶם יִרְבּוּ בַבָּר
יָצְאוּ וְלֹא־שָׁבוּ לָמוֹ׃

Who gave birth to the frost of heaven?
30 Water congeals like stone,
And the surface of the deep compacts.

31 Can you tie cords to Pleiades
Or undo the reins of Orion?
32 Can you lead out Mazzaroth[b] in its season,
Conduct the Bear with her sons?
33 Do you know the laws of heaven
Or impose its authority on earth?

34 Can you send up an order to the clouds
For an abundance of water to cover you?
35 Can you dispatch the lightning on a mission
And have it answer you, "I am ready"?
36 Who put wisdom in the hidden parts?
Who gave understanding to the mind?[c]
37 Who is wise enough to give an account of the heavens?
Who can tilt the bottles of the sky,
38 Whereupon the earth melts into a mass,
And its clods stick together.

39 Can you hunt prey for the lion,
And satisfy the appetite of the king of beasts?
40 They crouch in their dens,
Lie in ambush in their lairs.
41 Who provides food for the raven
When his young cry out to God
And wander about without food?

39 Do you know the season when the mountain goats give birth?
Can you mark the time when the hinds calve?
2 Can you count the months they must complete?
Do you know the season they give birth,
3 When they couch to bring forth their offspring,
To deliver their young?
4 Their young are healthy; they grow up in the open;
They leave and return no more.

[b] *Evidently a constellation.*
[c] *Or "rooster"; meaning of Heb. uncertain.*

5 מִי־שִׁלַּח פֶּרֶא חָפְשִׁי
וּמֹסְרוֹת עָרוֹד מִי פִתֵּחַ׃
6 אֲשֶׁר־שַׂמְתִּי עֲרָבָה בֵיתוֹ
וּמִשְׁכְּנוֹתָיו מְלֵחָה׃
7 יִשְׂחַק לַהֲמוֹן קִרְיָה
תְּשֻׁאוֹת נוֹגֵשׂ לֹא יִשְׁמָע׃
8 יְתוּר הָרִים מִרְעֵהוּ
וְאַחַר כָּל־יָרוֹק יִדְרוֹשׁ׃

9 הֲיֹאבֶה רֵּים עָבְדֶךָ
אִם־יָלִין עַל־אֲבוּסֶךָ׃
10 הֲתִקְשָׁר־רֵים בְּתֶלֶם עֲבֹתוֹ
אִם־יְשַׂדֵּד עֲמָקִים אַחֲרֶיךָ׃
11 הֲתִבְטַח־בּוֹ כִּי־רַב כֹּחוֹ
וְתַעֲזֹב אֵלָיו יְגִיעֶךָ׃
12 הֲתַאֲמִין בּוֹ כִּי־יָשׁוּב זַרְעֶךָ ישיב ק׳
וְגָרְנְךָ יֶאֱסֹף׃

13 כְּנַף־רְנָנִים נֶעֱלָסָה
אִם־אֶבְרָה חֲסִידָה וְנֹצָה׃
14 כִּי־תַעֲזֹב לָאָרֶץ בֵּיצֶיהָ
וְעַל־עָפָר תְּחַמֵּם׃
15 וַתִּשְׁכַּח כִּי־רֶגֶל תְּזוּרֶהָ
וְחַיַּת הַשָּׂדֶה תְּדוּשֶׁהָ׃
16 הִקְשִׁיחַ בָּנֶיהָ לְּלֹא־לָהּ
לְרִיק יְגִיעָהּ בְּלִי־פָחַד׃

17 כִּי־הִשָּׁהּ אֱלוֹהַּ חָכְמָה
וְלֹא־חָלַק לָהּ בַּבִּינָה׃
18 כָּעֵת בַּמָּרוֹם תַּמְרִיא
תִּשְׂחַק לַסּוּס וּלְרֹכְבוֹ׃

19 הֲתִתֵּן לַסּוּס גְּבוּרָה
הֲתַלְבִּישׁ צַוָּארוֹ רַעְמָה׃
20 הֲתַרְעִישֶׁנּוּ כָּאַרְבֶּה
הוֹד נַחְרוֹ אֵימָה׃
21 יַחְפְּרוּ בָעֵמֶק וְיָשִׂישׂ בְּכֹחַ
יֵצֵא לִקְרַאת־נָשֶׁק׃
22 יִשְׂחַק לְפַחַד וְלֹא יֵחָת
וְלֹא יָשׁוּב מִפְּנֵי־חָרֶב׃
23 עָלָיו תִּרְנֶה אַשְׁפָּה

5 Who sets the wild ass free?
Who loosens the bonds of the onager,
6 Whose home I have made the wilderness,
The salt land his dwelling-place?
7 He scoffs at the tumult of the city,
Does not hear the shouts of the driver.
8 He roams the hills for his pasture;
He searches for any green thing.

9 Would the wild ox agree to serve you?
Would he spend the night at your crib?
10 Can you hold the wild ox by ropes to the furrow?
Would he plow up the valleys behind you?
11 Would you rely on his great strength
And leave your toil to him?
12 Would you trust him to bring in the seed,
And gather it in from your threshing floor?

13 The wing of the ostrich beats joyously;
Are her pinions and plumage like the stork's?
14 She leaves her eggs on the ground,
Letting them warm in the dirt,
15 Forgetting they may be crushed underfoot,
Or trampled by a wild beast.
16 Her young are cruelly abandoned as if they were not hers;
Her labor is in vain for lack of concern.
17 For God deprived her of wisdom,
Gave her no share of understanding,
18 Else she would soar on high,
Scoffing at the horse and its rider.

19 Do you give the horse his strength?
Do you clothe his neck with a mane?
20 Do you make him quiver like locusts,
His majestic snorting [spreading] terror?
21 He[a] paws with force, he runs with vigor,
Charging into battle.
22 He scoffs at fear; he cannot be frightened;
He does not recoil from the sword.
23 A quiverful of arrows whizzes by him,

[a] *Lit. "They. . . ."*

לַהַב חֲנִית וְכִידוֹן׃
24 בְּרַעַשׁ וְרֹגֶז יְגַמֶּא־אָרֶץ
וְלֹא־יַאֲמִין כִּי־קוֹל שׁוֹפָר׃
25 בְּדֵי שֹׁפָר ׀ יֹאמַר הֶאָח
וּמֵרָחוֹק יָרִיחַ מִלְחָמָה
רַעַם שָׂרִים וּתְרוּעָה׃

And the flashing spear and the javelin.
24 Trembling with excitement, he swallows[b] the land;
He does not turn aside at the blast of the trumpet.
25 As the trumpet sounds, he says, "Aha!"
From afar he smells the battle,
The roaring and shouting of the officers.

26 הֲמִבִּינָתְךָ יַאֲבֶר־נֵץ
יִפְרֹשׂ כְּנָפָו לְתֵימָן׃ כנפיו ק׳
27 אִם־עַל־פִּיךָ יַגְבִּיהַּ נָשֶׁר
וְכִי יָרִים קִנּוֹ׃
28 סֶלַע יִשְׁכֹּן וְיִתְלֹנָן
עַל־שֶׁן־סֶלַע וּמְצוּדָה׃
29 מִשָּׁם חָפַר־אֹכֶל
לְמֵרָחוֹק עֵינָיו יַבִּיטוּ׃
30 וְאֶפְרֹחָו יְעַלְעוּ־דָם ואפרחיו ק׳
וּבַאֲשֶׁר חֲלָלִים שָׁם הוּא׃

26 Is it by your wisdom that the hawk grows pinions,
Spreads his wings to the south?
27 Does the eagle soar at your command,
Building his nest high,
28 Dwelling in the rock,
Lodging upon the fastness of a jutting rock?
29 From there he spies out his food;
From afar his eyes see it.
30 His young gulp blood;
Where the slain are, there is he.

מ
1 וַיַּעַן יְהוָה אֶת־אִיּוֹב וַיֹּאמַר׃

40 The Lord said in reply to Job:

2 הֲרֹב עִם־שַׁדַּי יִסּוֹר
מוֹכִיחַ אֱלוֹהַּ יַעֲנֶנָּה׃

2 [a]Shall one who should be disciplined complain against
Shaddai?[a]
He who arraigns God must respond.

3 וַיַּעַן אִיּוֹב אֶת־יְהוָה וַיֹּאמַר׃

3 Job said in reply to the Lord:

4 הֵן קַלֹּתִי מָה אֲשִׁיבֶךָּ
יָדִי שַׂמְתִּי לְמוֹ־פִי׃
5 אַחַת דִּבַּרְתִּי וְלֹא אֶעֱנֶה
וּשְׁתַּיִם וְלֹא אוֹסִיף׃

4 See, I am of small worth; what can I answer You?
I clap my hand to my mouth.
5 I have spoken once, and will not reply;
Twice, and will do so no more.

6 וַיַּעַן־יְהוָה אֶת־אִיּוֹב
מִנְ ׀ סְעָרָה וַיֹּאמַר׃ מן ק׳

6 Then the Lord replied to Job out of the tempest and
said:

7 אֱזָר־נָא כְגֶבֶר חֲלָצֶיךָ
אֶשְׁאָלְךָ וְהוֹדִיעֵנִי׃
8 הַאַף תָּפֵר מִשְׁפָּטִי
תַּרְשִׁיעֵנִי לְמַעַן תִּצְדָּק׃
9 וְאִם־זְרוֹעַ כָּאֵל ׀ לָךְ

7 Gird your loins like a man;
I will ask, and you will inform Me.
8 Would you impugn My justice?
Would you condemn Me that you may be right?
9 Have you an arm like God's?

b Or *"digs up."*

a-a *Meaning of Heb. uncertain.*

וּבְקוֹל כָּמֹהוּ תַרְעֵם׃
10 עֲדֵה־נָא גָאוֹן וָגֹבַהּ
וְהוֹד וְהָדָר תִּלְבָּשׁ׃
11 הָפֵץ עֶבְרוֹת אַפֶּךָ
וּרְאֵה כָל־גֵּאֶה וְהַשְׁפִּילֵהוּ׃
12 רְאֵה כָל־גֵּאֶה הַכְנִיעֵהוּ
וַהֲדֹךְ רְשָׁעִים תַּחְתָּם׃
13 טָמְנֵם בֶּעָפָר יָחַד
פְּנֵיהֶם חֲבֹשׁ בַּטָּמוּן׃
14 וְגַם־אֲנִי אוֹדֶךָּ
כִּי־תוֹשִׁעַ לְךָ יְמִינֶךָ׃

15 הִנֵּה־נָא בְהֵמוֹת אֲשֶׁר־עָשִׂיתִי עִמָּךְ
חָצִיר כַּבָּקָר יֹאכֵל׃
16 הִנֵּה־נָא כֹחוֹ בְמָתְנָיו
וְאֹנוֹ בִּשְׁרִירֵי בִטְנוֹ׃
17 יַחְפֹּץ זְנָבוֹ כְמוֹ־אָרֶז
גִּידֵי פַחֲדָו יְשֹׂרָגוּ׃ פחדיו ק׳
18 עֲצָמָיו אֲפִיקֵי נְחֻשָׁה ב״א נחושה
גְּרָמָיו כִּמְטִיל בַּרְזֶל׃
19 הוּא רֵאשִׁית דַּרְכֵי־אֵל
הָעֹשׂוֹ יַגֵּשׁ חַרְבּוֹ׃
20 כִּי־בוּל הָרִים יִשְׂאוּ־לוֹ
וְכָל־חַיַּת הַשָּׂדֶה יְשַׂחֲקוּ־שָׁם׃
21 תַּחַת־צֶאֱלִים יִשְׁכָּב
בְּסֵתֶר קָנֶה וּבִצָּה׃
22 יְסֻכֻּהוּ צֶאֱלִים צִלֲלוֹ
יְסֻבּוּהוּ עַרְבֵי־נָחַל׃
23 הֵן יַעֲשֹׁק נָהָר לֹא יַחְפּוֹז
יִבְטַח ׀ כִּי־יָגִיחַ יַרְדֵּן אֶל־פִּיהוּ׃
24 בְּעֵינָיו יִקָּחֶנּוּ
בְּמוֹקְשִׁים יִנְקָב־אָף׃
25 תִּמְשֹׁךְ לִוְיָתָן בְּחַכָּה
וּבְחֶבֶל תַּשְׁקִיעַ לְשֹׁנוֹ׃
26 הֲתָשִׂים אַגְמֹן בְּאַפּוֹ
וּבְחוֹחַ תִּקֹּב לֶחֱיוֹ׃
27 הֲיַרְבֶּה אֵלֶיךָ תַּחֲנוּנִים
אִם־יְדַבֵּר אֵלֶיךָ רַכּוֹת׃
28 הֲיִכְרֹת בְּרִית עִמָּךְ
תִּקָּחֶנּוּ לְעֶבֶד עוֹלָם׃
29 הַתְשַׂחֶק־בּוֹ כַּצִּפּוֹר

Can you thunder with a voice like His?
10 Deck yourself now with grandeur and eminence;
Clothe yourself in glory and majesty.
11 Scatter wide your raging anger;
See every proud man and bring him low.
12 See every proud man and humble him,
And bring them down where they stand.
13 Bury them all in the earth;
Hide their faces in obscurity.
14 Then even I would praise you
For the triumph your right hand won you.

15 Take now behemoth, whom I made as I did you;
He eats grass, like the cattle.
16 His strength is in his loins,
His might in the muscles of his belly.
17 [a]He makes his tail stand up[a] like a cedar;
The sinews of his thighs are knit together.
18 His bones are like tubes of bronze,
His limbs like iron rods.
19 He is the first of God's works;
Only his Maker can draw the sword against him.
20 The mountains yield him produce;
All the beasts of the field play there.
21 He lies down beneath the lotuses,
In the cover of the swamp reeds.
22 The lotuses embower him in shade;
The willows of the brook surround him.
23 He can restrain the river from its rushing;
He is confident the stream[b] will gush at his command.
24 Can he be taken by his eyes?
Can his nose be pierced by hooks?
25 Can you draw out Leviathan by a fishhook?
Can you press down his tongue by a rope?
26 Can you put a ring through his nose,
Or pierce his jaw with a barb?
27 Will he plead with you at length?
Will he speak soft words to you?
28 Will he make an agreement with you
To be taken as your lifelong slave?
29 Will you play with him like a bird,

[b] *Lit. "Jordan."*

וְתִקְשְׁרֶנּוּ לְנַעֲרוֹתֶיךָ׃
30 יִכְרוּ עָלָיו חַבָּרִים
יֶחֱצוּהוּ בֵּין כְּנַעֲנִים׃
31 הֲתְמַלֵּא בְשֻׂכּוֹת עוֹרוֹ
וּבְצִלְצַל דָּגִים רֹאשׁוֹ׃
32 שִׂים־עָלָיו כַּפֶּךָ
זְכֹר מִלְחָמָה אַל־תּוֹסַף׃ פתח בס"ם

And tie him down for your girls?
30 [a]Shall traders traffic in him?[a]
Will he be divided up among merchants?
31 Can you fill his skin with darts
Or his head with fish-spears?
32 Lay a hand on him,
And you will never think of battle again.

מא

1 הֵן־תֹּחַלְתּוֹ נִכְזָבָה
הֲגַם אֶל־מַרְאָיו יֻטָל׃
2 לֹא־אַכְזָר כִּי יְעִירֶנּוּ יעורנו ק׳
וּמִי הוּא לְפָנַי יִתְיַצָּב׃
3 מִי הִקְדִּימַנִי וַאֲשַׁלֵּם
תַּחַת כָּל־הַשָּׁמַיִם לִי־הוּא׃
4 לֹא־אַחֲרִישׁ בַּדָּיו לו ק׳
וּדְבַר גְּבוּרוֹת וְחִין עֶרְכּוֹ׃
5 מִי־גִלָּה פְּנֵי לְבוּשׁוֹ
בְּכֶפֶל רִסְנוֹ מִי יָבוֹא׃
6 דַּלְתֵי פָנָיו מִי פִתֵּחַ
סְבִיבוֹת שִׁנָּיו אֵימָה׃
7 גַּאֲוָה אֲפִיקֵי מָגִנִּים
סָגוּר חוֹתָם צָר׃
8 אֶחָד בְּאֶחָד יִגַּשׁוּ
וְרוּחַ לֹא־יָבֹא בֵינֵיהֶם׃
9 אִישׁ־בְּאָחִיהוּ יְדֻבָּקוּ
יִתְלַכְּדוּ וְלֹא יִתְפָּרָדוּ׃
10 עֲטִישֹׁתָיו תָּהֶל אוֹר
וְעֵינָיו כְּעַפְעַפֵּי־שָׁחַר׃
11 מִפִּיו לַפִּידִים יַהֲלֹכוּ
כִּידוֹדֵי אֵשׁ יִתְמַלָּטוּ׃
12 מִנְּחִירָיו יֵצֵא עָשָׁן
כְּדוּד נָפוּחַ וְאַגְמֹן׃
13 נַפְשׁוֹ גֶּחָלִים תְּלַהֵט
וְלַהַב מִפִּיו יֵצֵא׃
14 בְּצַוָּארוֹ יָלִין עֹז
וּלְפָנָיו תָּדוּץ דְּאָבָה׃
15 מַפְּלֵי בְשָׂרוֹ דָבֵקוּ
יָצוּק עָלָיו בַּל־יִמּוֹט׃
16 לִבּוֹ יָצוּק כְּמוֹ־אָבֶן
וְיָצוּק כְּפֶלַח תַּחְתִּית׃

41

See, any hope [of capturing] him must be disappointed;
One is prostrated by the very sight of him.
2 There is no one so fierce as to rouse him;
Who then can stand up to Me?
3 Whoever confronts Me I will requite,
For everything under the heavens is Mine.
4 [a]I will not be silent concerning him
Or the praise of his martial exploits.[a]
5 Who can uncover his outer garment?
Who can penetrate the folds of his jowls?
6 Who can pry open the doors of his face?
His bared teeth strike terror.
7 His protective scales are his pride,
Locked with a binding seal.
8 One scale touches the other;
Not even a breath can enter between them.
9 Each clings to each;
They are interlocked so they cannot be parted.
10 His sneezings flash lightning,
And his eyes are like the glimmerings of dawn.
11 Flames issue from his mouth;
Fiery sparks escape.
12 Out of his nostrils comes smoke
As from a steaming, boiling cauldron.
13 His breath ignites coals;
Flames issue from his mouth.
14 Strength resides in his neck;
Power leaps before him.
15 The layers of his flesh stick together;
He is as though cast hard; he does not totter.
16 His heart is cast hard as a stone,
Hard as the nether millstone.

a-a *Meaning of Heb. uncertain.*

17 מְשֵׂתוֹ יָגוּרוּ אֵלִים
מִשְּׁבָרִים יִתְחַטָּאוּ׃
18 מַשִּׂיגֵהוּ חֶרֶב בְּלִי תָקוּם
חֲנִית מַסָּע וְשִׁרְיָה׃
19 יַחְשֹׁב לְתֶבֶן בַּרְזֶל
לְעֵץ רִקָּבוֹן נְחוּשָׁה׃
20 לֹא־יַבְרִיחֶנּוּ בֶן־קָשֶׁת
לְקַשׁ נֶהְפְּכוּ־לוֹ אַבְנֵי־קָלַע׃
21 כְּקַשׁ נֶחְשְׁבוּ תוֹתָח
וְיִשְׂחַק לְרַעַשׁ כִּידוֹן׃
22 תַּחְתָּיו חַדּוּדֵי חָרֶשׂ
יִרְפַּד חָרוּץ עֲלֵי־טִיט׃
23 יַרְתִּיחַ כַּסִּיר מְצוּלָה
יָם יָשִׂים כַּמֶּרְקָחָה׃
24 אַחֲרָיו יָאִיר נָתִיב
יַחְשֹׁב תְּהוֹם לְשֵׂיבָה׃
25 אֵין־עַל־עָפָר מָשְׁלוֹ
הֶעָשׂוּ לִבְלִי־חָת׃
26 אֵת־כָּל־גָּבֹהַּ יִרְאֶה
הוּא מֶלֶךְ עַל־כָּל־בְּנֵי־שָׁחַץ׃

17 Divine beings are in dread as he rears up;
As he crashes down, they cringe.
18 No sword that overtakes him can prevail,
Nor spear, nor missile, nor lance.
19 He regards iron as straw,
Bronze, as rotted wood.
20 No arrow can put him to flight;
Slingstones turn into stubble for him.
21 Clubs[a] are regarded as stubble;
He scoffs at the quivering javelin.
22 His underpart is jagged shards;
It spreads a threshing-sledge on the mud.
23 He makes the deep seethe like a cauldron;
He makes the sea [boil] like an ointment-pot.
24 His wake is a luminous path;
He makes the abyss seem white-haired.
25 There is no one on land who can dominate him,
Made as he was without fear.
26 He sees all that is haughty;
He is king over all proud beasts.

מב
1 וַיַּעַן אִיּוֹב אֶת־יְהוָה וַיֹּאמַר׃

42 Job said in reply to the Lord:

2 יָדַעְתָּ כִּי־כֹל תּוּכָל ידעתי ק׳
וְלֹא־יִבָּצֵר מִמְּךָ מְזִמָּה׃
3 מִי זֶה ׀ מַעְלִים עֵצָה בְּלִי־דָעַת
לָכֵן הִגַּדְתִּי וְלֹא אָבִין
נִפְלָאוֹת מִמֶּנִּי וְלֹא אֵדָע׃
4 שְׁמַע־נָא וְאָנֹכִי אֲדַבֵּר
אֶשְׁאָלְךָ וְהוֹדִיעֵנִי׃
5 לְשֵׁמַע־אֹזֶן שְׁמַעְתִּיךָ
וְעַתָּה עֵינִי רָאָתְךָ׃
6 עַל־כֵּן אֶמְאַס וְנִחַמְתִּי פתח באתנח
עַל־עָפָר וָאֵפֶר׃

2 I know that You can do everything,
That no plan is impossible for You.
3 Who is this who obscures counsel without knowledge?
Indeed, I spoke without understanding
Of things beyond me, which I did not know.
4 Hear now, and I will speak;
I will ask, and You will inform me.
5 I had heard You with my ears,
But now I see You with my eyes;
6 Therefore, I recant and relent,
Being but dust and ashes.

7 וַיְהִי אַחַר דִּבֶּר יְהוָה אֶת־
הַדְּבָרִים הָאֵלֶּה אֶל־אִיּוֹב וַיֹּאמֶר
יְהוָה אֶל־אֱלִיפַז הַתֵּימָנִי חָרָה אַפִּי
בְךָ וּבִשְׁנֵי רֵעֶיךָ כִּי לֹא דִבַּרְתֶּם אֵלַי
8 נְכוֹנָה כְּעַבְדִּי אִיּוֹב׃ וְעַתָּה קְחוּ־
לָכֶם שִׁבְעָה־פָרִים וְשִׁבְעָה אֵילִים

7 After the Lord had spoken these words to Job, the Lord said
to Eliphaz the Temanite, "I am incensed at you and your two
friends, for you have not spoken the truth about Me as did My
servant Job. 8 Now take seven bulls and seven rams and go to My
servant Job and sacrifice a burnt offering for yourselves. And let

Job, My servant, pray for you; for to him I will show favor and not treat you as disgraced, since you have not spoken the truth about Me as did My servant Job." 9 Eliphaz the Temanite and Bildad the Shuhite and Zophar the Naamathite went and did as the LORD had told them, and the LORD showed favor to Job. 10 The LORD restored Job's fortunes when he prayed on behalf of his friends, and the LORD gave Job twice what he had before.

11 All his brothers and sisters and all his former friends came to him and had a meal with him in his house. They consoled and comforted him for all the misfortune that the LORD had brought upon him. Each gave him one *kesitah*[a] and each one gold ring. 12 Thus the LORD blessed the latter years of Job's life more than the former. He had fourteen thousand sheep, six thousand camels, one thousand yoke of oxen, and one thousand she-asses. 13 He also had seven sons and three daughters. 14 The first he named Jemimah, the second Keziah, and the third Keren-happuch. 15 One could not find anywhere in the land women as beautiful as Job's daughters. Their father gave them estates together with their brothers. 16 Afterward, Job lived one hundred and forty years to see four generations of sons and grandsons. 17 So Job died old and contented.

וּלְכ֞וּ | אֶל־עַבְדִּ֣י אִיּ֗וֹב וְהַעֲלִיתֶ֤ם
עוֹלָה֙ בַּֽעַדְכֶ֔ם וְאִיּ֣וֹב עַבְדִּ֔י יִתְפַּלֵּ֖ל
עֲלֵיכֶ֑ם כִּ֣י | אִם־פָּנָ֣יו אֶשָּׂ֗א לְבִלְתִּ֞י
עֲשׂ֤וֹת עִמָּכֶם֙ נְבָלָ֔ה כִּ֠י לֹ֣א דִבַּרְתֶּ֥ם
אֵלַ֛י נְכוֹנָ֖ה כְּעַבְדִּ֥י אִיּֽוֹב: 9 וַיֵּלְכוּ֩
אֱלִיפַ֨ז הַתֵּֽימָנִ֜י וּבִלְדַּ֣ד הַשּׁוּחִ֗י צֹפַ֤ר
הַנַּֽעֲמָתִי֙ וַיַּֽעֲשׂ֔וּ כַּֽאֲשֶׁ֛ר דִּבֶּ֥ר אֲלֵיהֶ֖ם
יְהֹוָ֑ה וַיִּשָּׂ֥א יְהֹוָ֖ה אֶת־פְּנֵ֥י אִיּֽוֹב:
10 וַֽיהֹוָ֗ה שָׁ֚ב אֶת־שְׁב֣וּת אִיּ֔וֹב
בְּהִֽתְפַּֽלְל֖וֹ בְּעַ֣ד רֵעֵ֑הוּ וַיֹּ֧סֶף יְהֹוָ֛ה
אֶת־כָּל־אֲשֶׁ֥ר לְאִיּ֖וֹב לְמִשְׁנֶֽה:
11 וַיָּבֹ֣אוּ אֵ֠לָיו כָּל־אֶחָ֨יו וְכָל־אַחְיֹתָ֜יו
וְכָל־יֹֽדְעָ֣יו לְפָנִ֗ים וַיֹּֽאכְל֨וּ עִמּ֣וֹ
לֶ֚חֶם בְּבֵית֔וֹ וַיָּנֻ֤דוּ לוֹ֙ וַיְנַֽחֲמ֣וּ אֹת֔וֹ
עַ֚ל כָּל־הָ֣רָעָ֔ה אֲשֶׁר־הֵבִ֥יא יְהֹוָ֖ה
עָלָ֑יו וַיִּתְּנוּ־ל֗וֹ אִ֚ישׁ קְשִׂיטָ֣ה אֶחָ֔ת
12 וְאִ֕ישׁ נֶ֥זֶם זָהָ֖ב אֶחָֽד: וַֽיהֹוָ֗ה בֵּרַ֛ךְ
אֶת־אַֽחֲרִ֥ית אִיּ֖וֹב מֵרֵֽאשִׁת֑וֹ וַֽיְהִי־ל֡וֹ
אַרְבָּעָה֩ עָשָׂ֨ר אֶ֜לֶף צֹ֗אן וְשֵׁ֣שֶׁת
אֲלָפִ֣ים גְּמַלִּ֔ים וְאֶֽלֶף־צֶ֥מֶד בָּקָ֖ר
13 וְאֶ֥לֶף אֲתוֹנֽוֹת: וַֽיְהִי־ל֛וֹ שִׁבְעָ֥נָה
14 בָנִ֖ים וְשָׁל֥וֹשׁ בָּנֽוֹת: וַיִּקְרָ֤א שֵׁם־
הָֽאַחַת֙ יְמִימָ֔ה וְשֵׁ֥ם הַשֵּׁנִ֖ית קְצִיעָ֑ה
15 וְשֵׁ֥ם הַשְּׁלִישִׁ֖ית קֶ֣רֶן הַפּֽוּךְ: וְלֹ֨א
נִמְצָ֜א נָשִׁ֥ים יָפ֛וֹת כִּבְנ֥וֹת אִיּ֖וֹב בְּכָל־
הָאָ֑רֶץ וַיִּתֵּ֨ן לָהֶ֧ם אֲבִיהֶ֛ם נַֽחֲלָ֖ה
16 בְּת֥וֹךְ אֲחֵיהֶֽם: וַיְחִ֤י אִיּוֹב֙ אַֽחֲרֵי־
זֹ֔את מֵאָ֤ה וְאַרְבָּעִים֙ שָׁנָ֔ה וַיִּרְאֶ֣ה אֶת־
בָּנָיו֙ וְאֶת־בְּנֵ֣י בָנָ֔יו אַרְבָּעָ֖ה דֹּרֽוֹת:
17 וַיָּ֤מָת אִיּוֹב֙ זָקֵ֖ן וּשְׂבַ֥ע יָמִֽים:

[a] *A unit of unknown value.*